T0305532

Rent Control

First Published in 1987, *Rent Control* discusses the economics of rent control citing numerous international examples of the detrimental effects of rigid rent control. Various policy options to revamp rental housing markets are examined critically. Rent control has proved a key issue in both politics and economics, repeatedly dividing interventionists and free marketeers. Consequently, its history - throughout the world- is extremely involved and tangled. Successive governments have sought to reverse the legislation of their predecessors without appearing, on the one hand, to remove the right to manage their own properties from landlords, or on the other to condone the behavior of unscrupulous and exploitative landlords. The authors argue that partial repeals of rent control have been ineffective at best, and counterproductive at worst. Only complete abolition of rent and eviction controls imposed by the state can bring about revitalised housing markets, and the book ends with a discussion of how this can be done without causing too much hardship. This is an interesting read for scholars and researchers of political economy and British economy.

Rent Control

Robert Albon and David C Stafford

First published in 1987
by Croom Helm

This edition first published in 2024 by Routledge
4 Park Square, Milton Park, Abingdon, Oxon, OX14 4RN

and by Routledge
605 Third Avenue, New York, NY 10017

Routledge is an imprint of the Taylor & Francis Group, an informa business

Publisher's Note
The publisher has gone to great lengths to ensure the quality of this reprint but points out that some imperfections in the original copies may be apparent.

Disclaimer
The publisher has made every effort to trace copyright holders and welcomes correspondence from those they have been unable to contact.

A Library of Congress record exists under ISBN: 0709954115

ISBN: 978-1-032-64610-7 (hbk)
ISBN: 978-1-032-64615-2 (ebk)
ISBN: 978-1-032-64613-8 (pbk)

Book DOI 10.4324/9781032646152

RENT
CONTROL

ROBERT ALBON and DAVID C. STAFFORD

CROOM HELM
London • New York • Sydney

© 1987 Robert Albon and David C. Stafford
Croom Helm Ltd, Provident House, Burrell Row,
Beckenham, Kent, BR3 1AT
Croom Helm Australia, 44-50 Waterloo Road,
North Ryde, 2113, New South Wales

Published in the USA by
Croom Helm
in association with Methuen, Inc.
29 West 35th Street
New York, NY 10001

British Library Cataloguing in Publication Data

Albon, Robert
  Rent control.
  1. Rental housing — Great Britain 2. Rent
  control — Great Britain
  I. Title II. Stafford, D.C.
  333.33′8   HD7288.85.G7

  ISBN 0-7099-5411-5

Library of Congress Cataloging-in-Publication Data

Albon, Robert, 1951-
  Rent control / Robert Albon and David C. Stafford.
      p.   cm.
  Bibliography: p.
  Includes index.
  ISBN 0-7099-5411-5
  1. Rent control — Great Britain. 2. Rent control. I. Stafford,
D.C. II. Title.
HD7288.85.G7A4   1987
363.5′6′0941 — dc19   87-15899

Printed and bound in Great Britain
by Billing & Sons Limited, Worcester.

CONTENTS

PREFACE

Our purpose in writing this book is to examine the theory and practice of rent control and contribute to the important debate on the future of the rented sector in Britain and elsewhere. We have assembled in this book a body of worldwide evidence that is fundamentally hostile to rent control. Wherever rent control has been imposed the effects have been at best adverse, and at worst, catastrophic. It is our opinion that it is high time that the British Government seized the nettle of decontrol. To relax the Rent Act totally has so far proved politically unacceptable. It is not enough that the Government merely shifts the goal posts to avoid radical reform. We advocate an early step by the Government to deregulate all new lettings made by landlords, rather than encouraging a certain amount of renovation by 'approved' landlords as under the Housing and Planning Act, 1986. We also argue strongly that it is feasible for the phasing in of deregulation for existing tenants without unacceptable hardship.

Private rented housing is falling both in absolute terms and as a percentage of the total housing stock. The number of privately rented homes in England has dwindled from 6 million in 1951 to 4.3 million in 1961 and 1.6 million in 1987. Extending home ownership through the sale of council houses has been one of the Conservative Government's greatest political successes but, to date, its policy towards rented housing has been one of its biggest failures. For a Conservative Government which eagerly abolished the preposterous Price Commission soon after it

Preface

took power in 1979, it has been singularly ineffective in facing up to the very real harm done by rent control. In particular, the Government's decision to step back from rent deregulation in 1985 ensured, among other adverse effects, that the continuing and growing shortage of rented housing would not only hinder mobility of labour at a time of high unemployment, but simply place yet more pressure on the public housing sector.

Crucial to any re-vamping of the private rental housing market is an economic return to landlords and this implies a decontrol of rents. The Government's early attempts at deregulation through the Assured Tenancy Scheme, introduced in 1980, whereby approved bodies can build for rent outside the rent regulation machinery has been a failure with only some 600 new homes built. The Government's latest proposal will allow local authorities to give grants to housing associations and other housebuilders to finance up to 30 per cent of a project, helping to cover the difference between rent revenue and construction cost. There is little evidence to believe that this scheme is likely to be any more successful than past pump priming schemes. It is unrealistic to think that there is an untapped source of private funds for investment in housing to rent when such schemes will not only require government approval but be open to political manipulation by local authorities. In short, such schemes could easily become a substitute for council housing rather than a real and commercially viable alternative.

Robert Albon
David C. Stafford

ABOUT THE AUTHORS

Dr Robert Albon lectures in economics at the Australian National University and has held visiting positions at Virginia Polytechnic Institute and State University, Monash University and (during 1986) the University of Birmingham. His main research interests are in the broad areas of applied and public microeconomics, and he has written extensively on subjects including housing economics (including a doctoral thesis on rental housing policy), issues relating to the regulation and behaviour of government-owned enterprises and taxation policy. His recent books and monographs include <u>Privatise the Post</u> (Centre for Policy Studies, 1987) and <u>Taxation Policy in the Eighties</u> (Allen & Unwin, 1986).

Dr David Stafford is Head of the Department of Economics and Senior Lecturer at the University of Exeter. He has acted as an economic consultant to Government Departments and to a number of financial institutions. His research interests are in the areas of public finance and expenditure and institutional finance and investment. His recent books have included <u>Open-end Investment Funds in the EEC and Switzerland</u> (Macmillan, 1977), <u>Economics of Housing Policy</u> (Croom Helm, 1978), <u>Bank Competition and Advertising</u> (The Advertising Association, 1982), <u>Key Developments in Personal Finance</u> (Basil Blackwell, 1985), <u>Directory of Unit Trust Management</u> (Stock Exchange Press, 1986), <u>Risk Ratio</u> (Practical Portfolio, 1987), and <u>Housing Finance and Policy</u> (Croom Helm, 1987).

INTRODUCTION

Our opposition to rent and eviction controls is clear and unequivocal. From our research into the effects of rental market controls in various parts of the world at various times, the same picture emerges. The effects on the quantity and quality of the housing stock can be devastating - similar to the impact of bombing according to one Swedish socialist economist. The controls also lead to an excess demand for housing which fosters unfortunate practices such as discrimination on various grounds other than willingness and ability to pay rent, and the creation of a black market. Further, rent and eviction controls have a major impact on the mobility of labour. The encouragement to immobility can lead to the perpetration of structural imbalances in a developing economy. These rigidities can have very large economic and social costs.

Our disapproval of rental market controls is on the basis of both economic and 'philosophical' considerations. We do not regard such intervention as either efficient or equitable in any senses of these two words. Consider first the efficiency of rental market controls.

The inefficiencies associated with rental market controls can be enormous. The standard welfare criterion used by economists is the 'Kaldor-Hicks' or 'potential Pareto' criterion. It states that an economic policy change is desirable if the gainers could compensate the losers while still remaining better off themselves. We make much use of this criterion in our assessment of rental market controls and of alternative ways of bestowing the

Introduction

same benefits on tenants. Such controls are, without doubt, the most costly and callous way to achieve this end of all the feasible alternatives.

We also argue that rent and eviction controls are 'unfair' in any sense of the word. The redistribution from rent control is a haphazard one - almost like randomly selecting donors and recipients of a subsidy from the telephone book. There is no evidence that either tenants are poor or landlords are rich in general. Some of each are rich and some are poor. Robin Hood would probably not find the pattern of enforced redistribution appealing.

Unfairness is also evident when the issue is looked at from another angle. Rent control is the only instance of a housing subsidy that is not provided by taxpayers in general - the burden falls on landlords. Compare this with rent rebates, council housing and tax deductibility of mortgage interest where the community funds the subsidies. We have the utmost opposition to those who argue for the perpetuation of rent control on the basis that it would be costly to government revenues to abolish it.

Many proposals that argue for the end of rental market controls involve compensation for sitting tenants, in some cases by enormous amounts - up to 10 years of the difference between market and controlled rents. We think that these are remarkably generous terms of compensation for the removal of something to which the tenant never had a 'right'. We are quite serious when we suggest that if either party is to receive compensation it should be the landlord and not the tenant. Rent control takes, forcibly, from the landlord and gives to the tenant. Decontrol returns to the landlord what was his but only after a period of deprivation. Who has lost and who has 'gained' by this?

Rights to one's property should be fundamental to a free society. That property should be protected by the state from theft or damage. The owner's right to sell, give away, hire or even destroy that property must be protected. If the owner wishes to enter a contract with another person so that the other person can have use of

vi

the property, under agreed conditions, the freedom of that contract must be respected. The state has a role in establishing a legal framework in which contractual rights and obligations can be agreed and enforced. Rental market controls are a clear violation of individual rights. Societies that impose such controls are stepping towards collectivism where private property is made 'public'.

The very idea that the state can give one person an 'interest' in the property of another, without his consent, is repugnant. And this is precisely what rent and eviction controls do. In a sense, they represent 'theft' by the state.

In addition to these 'economic' and 'philosophical' objections we also have a third reason for rejecting this kind of government interference. Controls on rents and evictions establish pressures for people to evade the law - they encourage illegal activity. Black markets replace, to some extent, legal ones. We feel that it is not wise to make laws that so obviously encourage evasion.

In making these remarks we do not wish to appear 'anti-tenant' or 'pro-landlord'. Our desire is to see the establishment (in Britain) and the maintenance (in many other places) of a healthy private rental market which is both efficient and equitable. Problems of low income should be viewed as being totally independent of the housing market and be dealt with separately. They are not, in any sense, the problem of the landlord.

Our overall purpose is to show that rental market controls inevitably have unintended adverse consequences irrespective of how well they are framed. Of course, the full set of controls is virtually never introduced in one action. More commonly, one control (e.g. on rents) is imposed, and this has consequences in the housing market. Legislators then react to these consequences by imposing further controls which, again, evoke reactions in the market. This interaction of controls and consequences results in a complex set of legislation which can prove a gold-mine for legal practitioners who can understand it. Perhaps the best example of the interactive process is that described by Cheung (1980) in his revealing paper on Hong Kong's rental market controls. We have attempted

Introduction

to capture the flavour of the process of legislative and market interaction in our Chapter One, 'The Tangled Web'. This provides a hypothetical example of the process as it often occurs and serves as a background to our discussions of the theory, empirical effects and policy considerations relating to rental market controls.

In Chapter Two, we give a brief overview of the theory of how the rental housing market works and how it is affected by the introduction of rent and eviction controls. The theoretical literature on these controls gives a clear indication of what can be expected - reductions in supply, deterioration of quality, non-price discrimination, black market dealings, inefficient use of dwelling space and immobility. It must be emphasised that these effects are unambiguous and that the basic analysis is agreed by virtually all economists. At least twenty textbooks could be cited which present this same basic analysis[1].

The effects on the rental housing market that are suggested by theoretical analysis are borne out by the factual evidence from all around the world. This evidence is reviewed in Chapters Three to Six. The international judgement on rent and eviction control is clear and unarguable. Even those who support rent control in some form or another concede the deleterious effects of rigid controls and either advocate a softer version (sometimes called 'rental market regulation' or 'rent review') or are prepared to accept the less pleasant costs and consequences for the sake of the perceived benefits received by tenants.

In Chapters Three and Four, we review the evidence on the effects of controls on the quantity and quality of rental housing available. In every instance - Paris, London, Glasgow, Sweden, San Francisco, New York, Melbourne, Sydney, Mexico City - the verdict is the same. No writer doubts this - rent and eviction control causes at least some landlords to exit the market, deters new ones from entering, results in inefficient use of house space, and usually leads to a run-down of maintenance. It is rare to find such unanimity on any question as on this one.

viii

Chapter Five examines the evidence that rent control causes an excess demand for rental housing where demand outstrips supply at the controlled rent. Associated with this we find a number of unpleasant practices develop although hard evidence is not always available. Landlords tend to discriminate between tenants on the basis of attributes such as race, general appearance, existence of children, etc. While these effects may occur in a free market, they are encouraged by rent and eviction control. Another consequence is the stimulus for illegal dealings - such as the payment of 'key-money' and above-rent payments - to take place in a 'black market'. This has been observed in many places at many times.

Chapter Six looks at the evidence on labour mobility and the use of available housing space. It is, as expected, common to notice that labour is less mobile when rent control is in force and that immobility also leads to an inefficient use of house space. The costs to society as a whole of these rigidities may be considerable. In the British context, the 'two nations' (north and south) division is exacerbated by rent control as well as other housing rigidities.

In Chapter Seven we divert our attention away from the experiences of other countries and focus on the British experience with rental market controls and abortive decontrol. Unlike other countries, Britain has never quite managed to rid itself of controls that were first introduced in 1915 as a temporary measure. Deregulation between the wars was reversed in the context of the second World War and these controls lingered on until abolition began in the late 1950s under a Conservative Government. These moves were reversed in the mid-1960s by a Labour Government and the controls were reinforced in the 1970s after a Conservative interlude. The present Government has taken only very limited steps towards decontrol and, in fact, the present Minister recently 'reaffirmed his commitment to maintaining the rent acts and emphasised the importance of political consensus if any changes in them were proposed' (Financial Times, 9.12.1986)[2].

Introduction

Of course, the controls on the rental housing market cannot be blamed totally for the decline in private renting in Britain. Both the encouragement of council housing and of owner-occupancy have played their part in killing this sector. Chapter Eight looks at these effects and describes the results of these policies combined with the Rent Acts - a small and sorry backwater of the housing market exhibiting many signs of decay and very few of life. This is in marked contrast to the position in many other countries where private renting is an important and 'respectable' segment of the housing market.

Chapter Nine reviews the various suggestions that have been made in regard to improving the situation, other than decontrol. 'Municipalisation' is one such proposal that used to receive attention. We also discuss various ways that 'reform' could occur within the existing legislative framework. Various possibilities have been put forward to retain controls but in a form that avoids some of the deleterious effects of the present controls.

Finally, in Chapter Ten, we put forward the case for decontrol and consider the various issues surrounding the mechanics of decontrol. In particular, we consider whether the rental market controls should be dismantled as a piecemeal measure or as part of a general overview of housing policy where all controls and subsidies are removed and any 'welfare' element replaced by a scheme of general income maintenance. This chapter also looks at any residual role for the state after the ending of heavy-handed rent and security of tenure restrictions.

Notes

1. Examples of the textbooks which include discussions of rental market controls are the standard texts used in many British universities (Begg, Fischer and Dornbusch, 1984 and Samuelson, 1980). Many widely used intermediate microeconomic textbooks (e.g. Call and Holahan, 1977; Hirshleifer, 1984, and McCloskey, 1985) and various applied microeconomics texts e.g. (Browning and Browning, 1983) and McKenzie and

Tullock, 1978) also contain sections on these types of controls.

2.   The Economist (3.1.1987) has listed four great failures under the Thatcher Government. One of these is the failure to revive the private rental housing market. It suggests that the Government should 'abolish all rent controls, instantly' (p.10).

CHAPTER ONE

THE TANGLED WEB

Rent control has ... constituted, maybe, the worst example of poor planning by governments lacking in courage and vision.

Gunnar Myrdal

In this chapter we trace the implications both in the market and in the administration of a 'typical' set of landlord and tenant provisions that control rents, evictions, conditions of tenancy, etc. This is not necessarily based on any particular piece of legislation. Rather it is a compendium of various interventions from different times and places. We find it convenient to begin with a single act of intervention - the control of residential dwellings rents - and to trace through the way landlords and tenants might react to this and the way that law-makers might respond to these reactions. While this is a hypothetical case study, it is contended that many actual cases exhibit most of the characteristics described.

As a consequence of the various actions and reactions to legislation relating to the rental housing market, a very complex picture can emerge. For this reason we have attempted to chart the 'tangled web' of effects in the market and in the legislature. This is presented as Figure 1.1 and, because every case is different, it is not quite the same story as that we are about to tell. A spider never weaves precisely the same web twice.

In our particular locality, a quite large city-state, the economy was enjoying a boom period with rising real disposable incomes and population. People were requiring

Figure 1.1: The tangled web of rent control

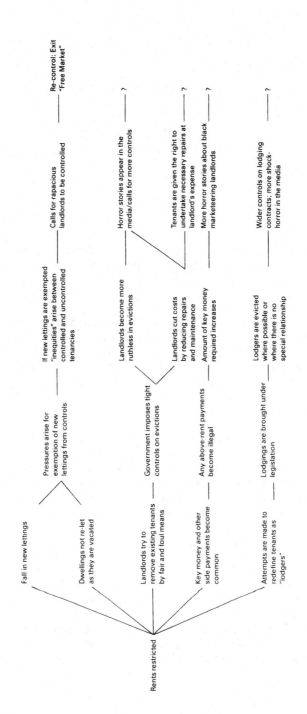

more and better housing of all kinds, including rented houses and flats. The availability of rented accommodation was growing at a rate below that of what people 'wanted' (in the sense of preparedness to pay) and this was putting upward pressure on rents which were, in fact, growing faster than prices in general. Some people were experiencing difficulties in finding accommodation at rents they could afford and this problem, popularly described as a 'housing shortage', was becoming an irritant to the Government. It was claimed by the Council of Social Services that private landlords were acting unreasonably in raising rents more rapidly than the inflation rate. Many less well-off people were suffering as a consequence of their avarice. The Council suggested that the Government should expand its programme of providing low-rent public housing and introduce a system of rigid rent control to stop the rise of private rents. The logic seemed impeccable to the Minister for Housing but there was a problem - it would be 'politically' difficult to increase spending on public housing. Rent control loomed as a 'cheap-fix' - a decisive action in response to a very visible problem. As prompt action was required there was no time for an investigation of the possible consequences or of other changes to the existing legislation, The Landlord and Tenant Act. This Act, basically provided for landlords and tenants to enter their own legally-binding contracts without interference from the state. The new Act, The Rent Restrictions Act, removed the right of landlords and tenants to set their own rents although all other elements of the contract remained unregulated.

The Act froze rents as of a certain date (six months in the past) for all residential tenancies in the city. It made it an offence to charge a rent greater than that which prevailed as of the particular prescribed date. All tenancy agreements made after the prescribed date were subject to a compulsory rent determination by a newly-appointed rent controller who was obliged to be cognisant of rents prevailing on comparable dwellings and of property value at the prescribed date in making his rent determinations. This meant that rents on newly-let resi-

3

dences were approximate to those that would have prevailed at the earlier prescribed date unless they were completely new residences. In this case the rent controller was obliged to estimate the property value that would have prevailed at the prescribed date, if it had existed, and base the rent on that figure. A considerable staff soon arose in the rent control office to process the numerous applications for determinations.

In a situation where 'market rents' were not subject to any upward pressure, this initial action would have little or no effect. However, rents were controlled in the context of rising market rents, where demand for accommodation was growing more quickly than supply. In these circumstances there will be reactions to the control by individual landlords and tenants.

The first reaction came when existing houses and flats became potentially available for rent through being vacated by the existing tenant or through changes in the circumstances of owners of existing residences (e.g. owner moving overseas temporarily, children leaving home). Normally (i.e. without rent restrictions) these houses would become available for rent but, under the changed circumstances, many owners thought twice. Perhaps they were better-off selling to an owner-occupier or even leaving the place vacant? The bottom line was that less existing accommodation was made available to tenants than otherwise.

Now consider the number of new dwellings constructed for letting. After a lag because of the considerable time needed to bring new places onto the market, investors in rental properties began to reassess the market potential. As construction costs were rising but rents were not, investors' anticipated rates of return fell and some scaled down or ceased their activities in the construction of new rental housing, favouring instead investment outlets where the returns were not regulated.

These two sets of reactions, with the same basic effect - lower than otherwise availability of accommodation - were matched by a demand-side response as more people were attracted to rental housing (or sought larger residences) as rents fell relative to people's incomes. This meant that there was a rental housing 'shortage' exacerbated from both the 'supply' and 'demand' sides. Some people seeking rental accommodation were unsuccessful even though they were willing to pay at least the going rent. This is what economists usually mean by a 'shortage'.

While there are always people who cannot pay the going rent, the peculiar phenomenon of rent control is the existence of people who are suitable prospective tenants who can pay the rent but cannot find a place to live. The shortage will manifest itself in various ways - dwindling 'To Let' advertisements and stories of dozens or even hundreds of enquiries about a single place are tell-tale signs. Estate agents will be in a particularly good position to see what is happening, as they act as an interface between landlords and tenants. Newspapers, radio and television will carry stories of homeless families. All of these signs emerged rather quickly in our case.

Other types of story also began to be told. Some landlords, their returns reduced by the rent control, found it attractive to rid themselves of their tenants and sell their properties to intending owner-occupiers. In the absence of controls on evictions (other than those contained in leases agreed by landlords and tenants and legally-enforceable), the only constraint on landlords not to eject tenants was a moral one. The media grasped onto stories about rapacious landlords ejecting 'innocent' tenants, sentencing them to homelessness or unsatisfactory accommodation.

On the other hand, home-hungry tenants began offering bribes of 'key-money' and/or above-controlled rent payments in order to secure tenancies. Many landlords were prepared to accept such payments, either from existing tenants (on the understanding that they would not be evicted) or from prospective tenants bidding for a vacant house or flat (or even for one currently tenanted). The 'black market' dealings became public knowledge, either by word-of-mouth or through media stories. Because the Rent Restriction Act had been so hastily framed it was not clear whether these activities were illegal or not.

The series of repercussions from the control of rents is not yet complete. The shortage of accommodation meant that frustrated tenants sought other means of attaining shelter - mobile homes, owner-occupancy and public housing provided a refuge for some. This spill-over created problems in these areas. For example, queues for the relatively cheap public housing tended to lengthen. Another area of accommodation was 'lodgings' where the landlord/lady provided some form of 'board', partial or full. This area has not been placed under control as yet and the growth of enquiries about lodgings tended to push up prices quite substantially. This gave another source of 'shock-horror' stories for the 'human interest' journalists.

The Government now found it had to act again. It was under pressure to 'do something' about the shortage of accommodation and black markets, 'wholesale' evictions and expensive lodgings. Rather than remove the root cause of the problems, the Government moved instead to plug up the holes in the leaky bucket. A special task force of the Ministry of Housing was charged with investigating the abuses of the Rent Restrictions Act and suggested ways of solving these problems. The principal recommendations of the Task Force were:

-   No evictions of tenants without an approved 'just cause'. Approved reasons were principally failure of the tenant to pay rent for a period of at least one month, wilful damage to the property and the requirement of the premises for the landlord's own use or that of his immediate family. Tenants had to be given period of notice ranging from one week to two months.

-   The imposition of severe penalties for a new set of offences relating to demands for, and acceptance of, above-rent payments to procure a tenancy.

-   The imposition of severe penalties for landlords who

discriminated in their selection of tenants on the basis of race, prospective tenants having children, etc.

- The bringing of lodgings under the 'protection' of the Act.

- The freeing of all new tenancies from the provisions of the Act with a requirement that each such tenancy be registered with the Residential Tenancies Office.

The Government accepted all the recommendations with the exception of the last after a strong representation from the Tenants Union who felt that such a move would be inequitable and would, in spite of the provisions relating to evictions, induce landlords to use foul methods of removing tenants so as to be able to re-let at a market rent. Further, it was felt that such a move was incompatible with the original intent of the legislation - that is, to 'allow access of tenants to privately-rented accommodation at fair and reasonable rents'.

In spite of these amendments the fundamental problems did not disappear - in fact, most of them got worse. Further, some new problems emerged. In particular, methods of eviction were becoming more unpleasant: 'key-money' was still rife, houses in some older areas were falling into disrepair and these types of problems were spreading to the lodgings area, although not to the same degree.

Landlords, now more desperate to get vacant possession and being unable to influence politicians to de-regulate rental housing, were reported to be using unsavoury means of trying to remove tenants. Where loopholes in the law could not be exploited, some landlords employed people to harrass tenants in various ways - phone calls late at night, veiled threats and other forms of intimidation. In some terrace houses there were 'walk-throughs' where a thug with a baseball bat under his coat would call at the house during the day and when the door was answered, brush past the hapless housewife, and walk through smashing furniture (but not damaging the house) before disappearing out the back door into the rear laneway. The difference between the value of a house without and with a sitting tenant was now about one quarter of the vacant possession value. A lot was at stake and, given that tenancies were deemed to be hereditary to immediate family, landlords saw nothing but a tip of an iceberg at the end of a very long tunnel.

Another reaction of landlords was to cut back on repairs and maintenance. The Government had been receiving many complaints from tenants about leaking roofs, broken windows not being repaired, unsatisfactory plumbing, etc. The Tenants Union was demanding that the Rent Restrictions Act be amended again to oblige landlords to carry out repairs or to allow tenants to have necessary repairs made and deduct the expenses from rent payments. The landlords' group, the Property Owners Association, was asking that the law be changed to empower the Rent Controller to set new rents on existing properties which take into account changes in free market property values, repair expenses and costs of insurance, rates, etc.

The Government, again under pressure to amend the legislation, decided that there was some merit in the landlords' appeal for the introduction of a formula for determining controlled rent levels but realised that the adoption of the landlords' suggested formula would effectively mean a major step towards decontrol. After much soul-searching (and lobbying from different groups) a compromise formula was reached. All rent determinations were now to have regard to current costs of repairs, insurance, local government rates, etc. However, determinations were still to be made on the basis of the property value at the time of the original rent control (now some 10 years earlier) in the case of applications regarding existing tenancies (landlords were allowed to apply for re-determinations on existing properties) while current values were to be used for any new tenancy agreements. Landlords were allowed to apply for a new determination no more than once every two years and when a property was re-let (or, of course, when a new or existing property first became available for rent). Tenancies for which current property values apply were placed on a special register to distinguish them from those under the 'old' rent control where original property values applied.

This very brave and controversial move represented the first step towards decontrol. Rents on all new lettings were not quite 'market rents' but they were close to those that would have prevailed without regulation. There was even some speculation that the Government may completely decontrol these new tenancies and look at ways to free-up the old rent control a little. The interesting thing was that the direction of change had shifted from one of increasingly greater control towards decontrol.

There was some improvement in regard to repairs. Landlords subject to old control could now redeem repair and maintenance expenses in higher rents. Previously some had had money outgoings in excess of rent receipts and while they were still a long way from getting anything like a market return on the funds tied up in their properties, the situation was a bit better. However, a vast number of properties were trapped in the old control.

The difference between 'old' and 'new' controlled rents could be very large. Dwelling A in a Typical Street under old control could be subject to a rent of less than half of Dwelling B next door which was identical except that it was subject to new control. This 'inequity' was a constant irritant to tenants' groups and landlords. Other inequities also began to show-up. One of the most important was that many tenants under old control had prospered over the years, partly as a consequence of their low housing costs, and were now in some cases much richer than their landlords. The ostentatious showing of their wealth (through e.g. 'flashy' cars at the front of the controlled property) was galling to their landlords who, on some occasions, resorted to desperate means of removing them.

The Tangled Web

The Government was still in a very difficult position. It was now beginning to see that there were still big problems - many tenants under old control could afford to pay market rents while others could not easily make the adjustment, especially after many years of experience of having rising incomes and no rises in rents being built-in to their expectations. Many, of course, were simply poor. As a group the old sitting tenants were a most formidable political force - the Government was scared to act and did not really know how to act in the absence of total decontrol. It could not see an easy way of adjusting the rent-setting formula that would result in partial movement towards market levels. Without knowing where to go it did as almost any government would do in the circumstances - it set up a Royal Commission into the operation of the Rent Restriction Act, as amended.

The Royal Commission created a forum for all the interested parties to voice their views. The Tenants' Union, the Property Owners' Association, the Estate Agents' Institute, the Law Society, various welfare groups, economists, valuers, etc., all had their say. The deliberations took some two years giving the Government some valuable breathing-space from having to make decisions - 'the matter is currently under review'. Finally, the Report of the Royal Commission was tabled in Parliament and its findings and suggestions revealed.

The Report's principal recommendation can be summarised in one word - 'decontrol'. Any problems of poverty were, it argued, the responsibility of Government, not of private landlords. If people cannot afford private market rents they require public subsidy or should be accommodated in public housing. The only way to restore vitality to the private rented housing sector is to create an environment conducive to investment. It argued that even the new rent control system had not worked completely satisfactorily because many landlords and potential landlords were scared that they might be subjected to more rigid controls. Of course, the Report argued, tenants should be protected from arbitrary eviction and should have access to rent-setting machinery in cases where rapacious landlords set 'above-market' rents. In these cases the Rent Controller would be obliged to have regard to current property values and rates-of-return and current costs of outgoings - his/her job was really one of setting a rent that was not out of line with those on comparable premises.

The Government took some time over the Report and finally came out with a set of changes that did not coincide with the Report's recommendations but did make some significant changes to the Act (including changing its name to the Residential Tenancies Act). The changes were as follows:

- The complete removal of any restrictions on rents charged for any new lettings and for those registered (i.e. those controlled tenancies not under the old control).

- The creation of a new category of uncontrolled tenancies where values for rating purposes exceeded a particular sum such that they were classed as 'luxury' apartments or houses. In these cases the landlord could immediately apply for release from the provisions of the old control.

- The introduction of what came to be known as the 'wealthy tenant' provision, where, if a tenant could be shown to have the means of providing his/her own accommodation, he/she could be asked to pay a rent 'approved' by the Rent Controller or be required to vacate the premises.

- The complete decontrol of lodgings, an area which it had proved difficult to administer.

It was now many years since the original rent control legislation had been introduced and as a consequence of the two major acts of decontrol and the natural attrition of 'old tenants', the uncontrolled market was beginning to act in a 'normal' manner, side-by-side with the dwindling, but still substantial, controlled sector. The old control still had its problems - and was still a source of that 'human interest' story on an off-day for journalists - but it was seen as a problem that would gradually disappear. More attention began to be directed to the unregulated segment of the market.

The Tenants Union that represented the 'old' tenants was a dying force and a new organisation of tenants - the Residential Lessee's Association (RLA) - began to attract attention. With strong influence from the consumer protectionist movement, the Association highlighted various problems in private tenancies - for example, some tenants had problems retrieving security deposits at the end of their tenancies; rents in some areas had risen dramatically and some landlords were rather shy about doing repairs while others were too obtrusive. The RLA called for an inquiry into the operation of the private rented sector (excluding the controlled sector) a call that was answered by the Government. The Government set up a broadly-representative 'community committee' to prepare a report on the situation and to make recommendations as to 'reform' of the existing legislation.

The Committee's report, A Fair Deal for Tenants, was a glossy production with photographs of derelict houses and impoverished people (sometimes on the street with their few possessions) and liberally sprinkled with cartoons featuring rapacious landlords (big cigars and flashy cars) and the meek poor. The report chronicled various malpractices and rent movements which 'proved' that the private rental housing market is inefficient and inequitable. There was no overall assessment of the market, simply a drawing of general inferences from a few cases. A detailed programme of legislative reform was set out.

The centre-point of the 'Fair Deal' was the concept of a 'fair rent'. Where a tenant (or a landlord) was unhappy with the prevailing rent, an application could be made to the Rent Arbiter for a binding fair rent determination. This rent was conceived of as that that would prevail for the particular dwelling in its particular locality if there were no shortage of accommodation in the area. This would, it was claimed, provide a reasonable rate-of-return to the landlord because it removed only what Jane Fonda has called the 'greed quotient' from rents i.e. the element exploiting a housing shortage. The determination of fair rents created a big problem for the Rent Arbiter because current property values could not be used as a basis if there was a housing shortage. The difficulty of translating this conception of a fair rent into a figure was overlooked by the community committee.

The other items in the committee's package included a strenthening of the controls on evictions; the reinforcement of the anti-discrimination provisions in the Residential Tenancies Act; the introduction of controls on the size and conditions for return of security deposits, and the introduction of a tenant's right to undertake necessary repairs and to deduct the cost from rent payments.

At the present time the Community Committee's suggestions are under consideration by the Government. The matter is receiving considerable attention in the media. An economist has written a review of the likely impact of the changes on the rental market and has drawn attention to the anomalies in the fair rent concept and the rather subtle adverse effects on the market that may ensue from the provisions. The unintended consequences of the amendments to the Act have also been highlighted by the Property Owners' Association and the Estate Agents' Institute. The Estate Agents' representative on the Community Committee has been publicly criticised by the Institute for being party to a report that makes recommendations contrary to its stated policy.

Whether the new-new control will get off the ground remains an open question.

CHAPTER TWO

THEORETICAL EFFECTS OF RENT CONTROL

An economist making a snap judgement on a topic as complex as rent control would clearly be acting irresponsibly. But how much more rash is a government that imposes such controls ... without analysis to support the move.

Steven Cheung

In our analysis of the general consequences of rent control two models with restrictive assumptions are elaborated. The first model employs a neoclassical but ad hoc conventional supply and demand analysis of the effects of control in the short and long terms under the assumption of homogeneous units and sites with a control system that imposes a ceiling on the rent of the dwelling units. The second model of the rented housing market assumes that homogeneous housing services, rather than homogeneous housing units, are traded in the market and also specifically distinguishes between the short and the long run.

While our two models elucidate many of the aspects of rental market controls, they are not sufficiently rich to cover all the implications of this type of interference in the market. This chapter also contains brief discussions of two other aspects of rental market controls - the effects in related markets and the consequences of controls for mobility.

While both the models in this chapter are simple and 'partial-equilibrium' in character, we contend that they capture the fundamental elements of the rental housing

15

Theoretical Effects of Rent Control

market and how it will react to controls on rents and evictions. The predictions that we draw from these models often conflict with those drawn from more informal analysis of the effects of rental market controls. We feel that it is very important to have a formal framework or 'model' as a background to a discussion of intervention in any market.

Simple Equilibrium Model

Consider first the standard textbook analysis of the effects of rental market controls.

Implied within a simple neoclassical equilibrium housing model (Figure 2.1) of the short and long run effects of rent control would be the following assumptions:

a)   all dwelling units are homogeneous and have the same site values; that is the level of housing services yielded by each dwelling unit is not variable;

b)   the rental market for dwelling units is perfectly competitive;

c)   the market demand curve DD for dwelling units slopes downwards;

d)   the market supply curve SS for dwelling units slopes upwards on the presumption of increasing costs. Since the market model is not derived from an explicit model of the firm, no specific reference is made to whether SS represents short or long run. More realistically, SS may be presumed to be perfectly inelastic in the short run, on the grounds that the number of dwellings units cannot be altered due to (i) the smallness of annual production in relation to total market stock, (ii) the spatial immobility of houses, and (iii) the high capital/output ratio of housing.

In Figure 2.1, it is assumed that the market is in equilibrium with Q_0 dwelling units and a rent of P_0 each. A

Theoretical Effects of Rent Control

Figure 2.1

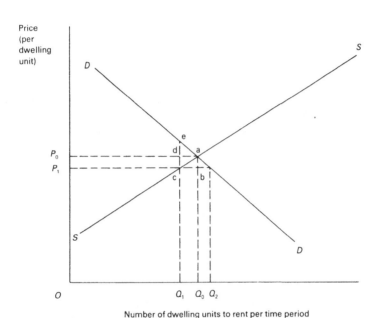

Number of dwelling units to rent per time period

ceiling rent of P_1 which is below the equilibrium rent of P_0 for all dwelling units is then applied. It might be considered more realistic to postulate the freezing of rents at P_0, and then to examine the effects of an increase in demand (for example, increased household formation) on the housing market. This approach is adopted by Lindbeck (1967) but does involve explicit assumptions on the price elasticity of supply in the short and long run.

Theoretical Effects of Rent Control

As a result of the imposition of P_1, the model yields a number of important predictions for the short run:

a)   the number of occupied dwelling units will decline to Q_1;

b)   there will be excess demand of $Q_2 - Q_1$ dwelling units. Such excess demand can lead to any one, or all, of the following consequences;[1]

   (i) non-price rationing (tenant discrimination), (ii) increased owner-occupation, (iii) the development of black markets, (iv) increased demand for housing in other rental sectors (local authority housing), (v) multiple accommodation, and (vi) increased home-lesseness;

c)   There will be a transfer from landlords to tenants of area $P_0 dcP_1$ and deadweight losses of economic surplus of ead (loss in tenants' surplus) and dac (loss in landlords' surplus).

d)   any subsequent increase in demand will lead to increased excess demand, but would not affect the number or rent of dwelling units;

e)   any increase in landlord costs will shift the supply curve upwards and lead to a further reduction in dwelling units offered for rent.

In the long run the effects will be more pronounced than in the short run. The long run supply curve will tend to be more elastic with respect to rents i.e. it will be 'flatter'.[2] This is because landlords have more options open to them in the long run. Under rent control more of them will remove their properties from private renting so that there will be fewer dwellings let, greater excess demand, etc. Indeed, in our simple model, the setting of a rent ceiling below the minimum long run average cost of the least-cost landlord would result in the extinction of

18

the private rental market.

The incentive for landlords to exit the industry, perhaps completely, is normally anticipated by legislators who usually combine rent controls with restrictions on evictions. Consider again Figure 2.1 where all initial Q_0 tenancies are now protected by security of tenure provisions in the legislation. Actual quantity of dwelling units does not change, but the lower rent (P_1) induces demand of Q_2 so that there is still an excess demand but now of only Q_2-Q_0. The consequences are, in this case, less pronounced than under rent control alone, although landlords suffer more.

The transfer from landlords to tenants is now P_0abP_1, compared with P_0dcP_1 under rent control alone. The deadweight losses of landlords' and tenants' surplus under rent control (dac and ead, respectively) disappear under the rigid form of rent and eviction control. In one sense this all looks rather nice.

The situation with rent and eviction controls looks better for everyone except, of course, landlords. However, this impression draws attention to the simplicity of our basic analysis.

Even within the confines of the model, imagine that there was an increase in demand for housing. This immediately results in a return of the deadweight losses and an increase in excess demand as there will be no supply response at all. Society will be deprived of the production of units of housing that are worth more to society than what they cost to produce.

Explicit Model of the Firm with Quality Variable

This model, developed by Frankena (1975) achieves a greater reality for policy prescriptions in the face of rent control, for it not only incorporates an explicit model of the individual firm which provides housing services, but distinguished between the short and long run adjustment period, and allows quality to be a variable. The specific assumptions are that:

a) homogeneous housing services are traded in the per-

19

fectly competitive rental market, rather than the services of homogeneous housing units as in the previous model (see Olsen, 1969 a,b);

b) the long run market supply curve, S_1S_1, is perfectly elastic since all firms have the same minimum long run average cost (LRAC);

c) the short run market supply curve, S_2S_2, is constructed by summing the short run firm supply curves in Figure 2.2;

d) the short run is defined as the period where no new firms can enter or exit the market and existing firms can only adjust quality, but some costs are fixed. Figure 2.2, incorporates the short run average cost curve (SRAC), the average variable cost (AVC), and the short run marginal cost (SRMC). These have the shapes conventionally assumed in microeconomic analysis.

In Figure 2.2, it is assumed that initially the firm is in equilibrium producing q_0 housing and operating at zero profits (i.e. 'normal' profits only) and that the market for housing services is in long run equilibrium, so that Q_0 units of housing services are traded at a rent of p_0 per unit.

As a result of a maximum rent of p_1 price per unit of housing services, the model yields the following predictions:

(a) <u>Decline in housing services</u>
In the model the representative profit-maximising firm will allow its dwelling units to deteriorate until the flow of housing services declines from q_0 to q_1 in Figure 2.2, and the aggregate output of housing services will decline from Q_0 to Q_1 in Figure 2.3. Any resulting lack of maintenance and repair is worsened by the landlord's uncertainty as to whether he will be able to repossess the property given that provisions exist in respect of tenants'

20

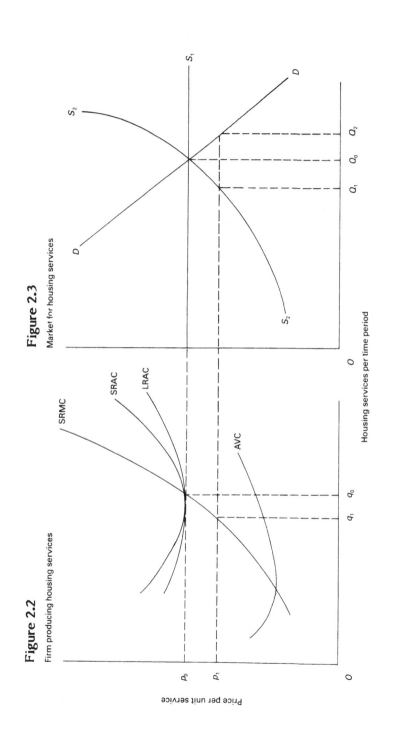

Figure 2.2

Firm producing housing services

Figure 2.3

Market for housing services

Theoretical Effects of Rent Control

security of tenure. Full analysis of the longer term effects on quality would require an even more complex model.

(b) Rents are depressed below market levels
In the model, since the price per unit of housing service will decline from p_0 to p_1, the rent per dwelling unit will also decline, because both the number of units of housing service per dwelling unit and the price per unit of housing service will decline.

(c) Excess demand for accommodation
In the model, there will be excess demand of Q_2-Q_1 units of housing service. Rent control poses a problem for potential new entrants to the market and for existing tenants who want to move. In such a restricted market, the cost of searching for accommodation can be very considerable, with complex effects on the welfare of the potential tenant. Again, a more complex model is required to explore the effects.

(d) Rise in costs will depress housing services
In the model, any increase in the demand for housing services will increase excess demand, and any increase in variable costs after the imposition of rent control will cause a further decline in housing services for the reasons discussed above.

(e) Landlords subsidise tenants
Rent restrictions have obvious implications for income distribution. To the extent that tenants pay low rents below the market price they are in effect receiving a subsidy from landlords. This is clearly a random distribution of income from landlord to tenants without regard to the financial circumstances of either. If the state really believes that tenants should be subsidised, it should ask if it should be the landlord or the state who should be responsible for this subsidy.

22

(f) Landlords leave market

The model predicts that all dwelling units existing at the time rent control is imposed would be, in the long run, withdrawn from the market. This assumed no decontrol takes place when properties are vacated. Thus, unless there are barriers to obtaining vacant possession, such as the strict security of tenure provision currently existing in Britain, the model predicts that under conditions of a perfectly competitive market, all properties will be eventually withdrawn from the market.

Analysis of 'Related Markets'

Obviously it is important to trace the 'general-equilibrium' implications of controls. Our two models are both partial-equilibrium and do not explore what happens in other markets. But we need to know where the excess demand goes and how this affects other related markets such as owner-occupancy and public renting. This analysis is beyond the scope of our book and, apart from the aspect examined in this section, we can give no more than the 'flavour' of the results at those points where the issue arises.

One important issue in regard to related markets is to determine whether rental levels in an uncontrolled market can be used to predict what would prevail in the controlled market if it were deregulated. This question becomes important when, say, new lettings are not controlled while old lettings remain under control. Is it the case that the excess demand from the controlled market 'spills over' into the uncontrolled, resulting in higher rents in the free market? Many commentators have argued that it would and have cautioned against using free market rents to predict what would happen after decontrol. For example, Paish (1952) and Needleman (1965) have made this claim in respect of rent controls.

The analysis in Albon (1981, Ch.2) gives a contrary view. Where there is freedom of entry into the uncontrolled segment of the market and there is no fear that controls will be extended to the free market, the long run rental level should be precisely equal to the market rent that would prevail if the whole market were free. Landlords could not sustain rents above this level because to do so would attract new entry that would compete rents down. However, it must be emphasised that this result holds only in the long run and where there is no fear of recontrol. Landlords would be coy about committing themselves if they feared extension of controls and this would result in higher rents incorporating a 'risk factor'.

Immobility
It is obvious that rental market controls are an immobilising factor. This is for two broad reasons. On the one hand, tenants under rent control are more reluctant to leave a tenancy than they would be if they were paying the full market rent. The holding of rent below its market level results in a tenant benefit which induces the occupant to stay on. Secondly, the excess demand created by rent control makes alternative accommodation more difficult to find. Both effects induce sitting tenants to sit.

This consequence can be costly to society as a whole for at least two reasons. Firstly, the functioning of the labour market is retarded as housing concerns restrict the free movement of workers from job-to-job. As we note in Chapter 6, this can be very costly indeed. Secondly, the efficiency of the use of house space can be adversely affected as tenants fail to move when their circumstances (e.g. family size) change. The longer rental market controls prevail the greater will be the mis-matching of people and houses. Again this is taken up in Chapter 6.

Conclusion
Rent controls can provide relief for sitting tenants, but prospective tenants and those existing tenants wishing to move can be very adversely affected in the long run. Landlords denied an economic return will sell as soon as an opportunity presents itself and invest elsewhere. Frequently, however, the landlord is locked in and undermaintains his property leading to premature decay and clearance. Low rents encourage the overconsumption of

house room since there is no incentive to economise. Finally, all tenants, and also landlords, rich or poor, are treated alike.

Far from promoting distributive justice, theoretical models of the housing market predict that rent controls:

- create and perpetuate housing shortages

- foster geographical immobility of tenants and prospective tenants

- limit consumer choice

- divert scarce resources towards other less valuable economic activities (i.e. create 'deadweight losses')

- encourage reduction in housing services, stock dilapidation and deter landlords from renting.

The fact that a formalised rent regulation machinery has now existed for over twenty years and that no government has yet been prepared to abolish it might almost lead even the gullible to believe that restriction of contractual terms and the setting of maximum rents will yield a greater amount of housing for a greater number of people than a free market could ever offer. Of course, the reverse has quite plainly been the case. The evidence offered by economic studies of the various adverse effects on housing supply arising from rent control will now be examined. In Chapter 3, we examine the effects of control on the stock of housing. Chapter 4, also explores the effects on supply by assessing the impact on the quality of housing and housing services. In Chapter 5, the way rent control creates excess demand and the consequences are explored. In Chapter 6, the effect of rent control on labour mobility is examined and the very serious repercussions of this are reviewed.

Theoretical Effects of Rent Control

Notes

1. The establishment of these consequences require a
    more sophisticated model than that which we have
    used. The simple model we have set out cannot
    generate these effects without modification and
    extension.

2. In fact, under our assumptions, the long run supply
    curve will be horizontal or 'perfectly elastic'.

CHAPTER THREE

HOUSING SHORTAGE

If educated people can't or won't see that fixing a price below the market level inevitably creates a 'shortage' (and one above a 'surplus'), it is hard to believe in the usefulness of telling them anything whatever in this field of discourse.

Professor Frank Knight,
Chicago School of Economics

For as long as rent controls have existed there have been economists critical of their introduction, perpetuation and consequences for the housing stock and its quality. In this chapter, we are particularly concerned with the effects of rent control on the size of the stock of housing and who actually received the available stock. In other words, we will use case studies to show the effects on the amount and efficiency in the use of housing space when rent controls are applied.

The Consequences of Shortage

Friedman and Stigler (1946), in their analysis of the effects of rent control in the USA begin with a salutary tale of market provision in spite of the appalling consequences of the San Francisco earthquake at the beginning of this century. They describe how the San Francisco earthquake of 1906 was followed by great fires which in three days destroyed 3400 acres of buildings in the city centre. According to a commander of the Federal troops, 'Not a hotel of note or importance was left standing. The

Housing Shortage

great apartment houses had vanished... Two hundred and twenty-five thousand people were... homeless.' Apparently a city of some 400,000 people lost over half its housing facilities. Of course, various factors did mitigate the acute shortage of housing. People left the city, some estimates go as high as 75,000. Temporary camps cared for perhaps as many as 30,000 people. Moreover, new construction and repair proceeded rapidly. What is significant, according to Friedman and Stigler, is that for many months after the disaster, it was necessary for some 20 per cent of the city's former population to be absorbed into the remaining half of the housing facilities. That is, each remaining house on average had to shelter 40 per cent more people. Yet, in the pages of the local newspaper, the San Francisco Chronicle of 24 May 1906, the first available issue after the earthquake, there is not a single mention of any housing shortage.

In fact, as Friedman and Stigler point out, classified advertisements listed 64 offers (some for more than one dwelling) of flats and houses for rent, and 19 houses for sale, against 5 advertisements of flats or houses wanted. Then and thereafter a considerable number of all types of accommodation except hotel rooms were offered for rent.

In contrast to the shortage of 1906, Friedman and Stigler examine the housing shortage of 1946 which was nationwide and included San Francisco. Because of the migration westward it was worse than average. In 1940, San Francisco's population of 635,000 had no housing shortage in the sense that only 93 per cent of the dwelling units were occupied. By 1946, the population had increased by at most a third - some 200,000.

At the same time, the number of dwelling units had increased by at least 20 per cent. In short, the city had to shelter 10 per cent more people in each dwelling unit than before the war. As Friedman and Stigler calculate, the shortage in 1946 was one quarter as acute as in 1906, when each remaining dwelling unit had to shelter 40 per cent more people than before the earthquake.

Friedman and Stigler emphasise that the housing shortage of 1946 did not pass unnoticed. On 8 January

28

1946, the Governor described the housing problem as 'the most critical problem facing California'. However, during the first five days of 1946 there were altogether only four advertisements offering houses or apartments for rent, as compared with 64 in one day in May 1906, and more advertisements offering to exchange housing in San Francisco for housing elsewhere. By contrast, in 1946, there were thirty advertisements per day by persons wishing to rent, against only five in 1906 after that disaster. During the same period in 1946, there were about sixty advertisements per day of houses for sale, as against nineteen in 1906.

Friedman and Stigler then conclude this comparative analysis of the two shortages in San Francisco in 1906 and 1946. They pose the question of how a relatively fixed amount of housing can be divided, i.e. rationed, among people, who wish for much more housing, until new construction can fill the gap? In 1906, the rationing was done by higher rents. In 1946, the use of higher rents to ration housing was made illegal by the imposition of rent ceilings, and the rationing was by chance and favouritism. A third possibility advanced by Friedman and Stigler would be for some sort of housing agency to undertake the rationing.

Using the empirical data available on the shortages of 1906 and 1946, Friedman and Stigler provide a perceptive piece of analysis of the comparative merits of the consequences on supply of two alternative rationing devices, (i) rationing by price, (ii) and rationing by chance and favouritism.

(i)   Rationing by Price
The authors consider it a superficial view whereby war experience has led many people to think of rationing as equivalent to coupons and order books. In fact, this type of rationing, although prevalent even in peacetime, is small in comparison with rationing through auction sale, i.e. rationing by price.

In the words of Friedman and Stigler,

Housing Shortage

> ... if demand for anything increases, competition among buyers tends to raise the price. The rise in price causes buyers to use the article more sparingly, carefully and economically, and thereby reduces consumption to the supply. At the same time, the rise in price encourages producers to expand output. Similarly, if demand for any article decreases, the price tends to fall, expanding consumption to the supply and discouraging output.

(Friedman and Stigler, 1946)

This mechanism is well illustrated, according to Friedman and Stigler when, in 1906, San Francisco used the free market method to deal with its housing problems, with a consequent rise of rents. They deduce some key advantages arising from rationing by higher rents:

1. In a free market, there is always some housing immediately available for rent - at all rent levels

2. The bidding up of rents forces some people to economise on space. Until there is sufficient new construction, this doubling up is the only solution.

3. The high rents act as a strong stimulus to new construction.

4. No complex, expensive, and expansive machinery is necessary. The rationing is conducted quietly, and impersonally through the price system.

(Friedman and Stigler, 1946)

In their empirical evidence Friedman and Stigler provide strong repudiations through offsetting and frequently advanced objections to free housing markets:

(a) 'The rich will get housing, and the poor none'

At all times during the acute 'shortage' of housing in 1906, Friedman and Stigler point out that inexpensive flats and houses were available. What is evident is that under free market conditions, the better housing will go to those who pay more, either because they have larger incomes or more wealth, or because they prefer better housing to, say, better cars. But, in the view of Friedman and Stigler, this fact had no more relation to the housing problem of 1946 than to that of 1940:

> If inequality of income and wealth among individuals justifies rent controls in 1946, it provided an even stronger reason for such controls in 1940. The danger, if any, that the rich would get all the housing was even greater in 1940 than in 1946.

(Friedman and Stigler, 1946)

The authors argue that each person or family was using in 1946 at least as much housing space, on the average, as before the war. Moreover, the total income of the USA was distributed in 1946 more equally among the country's families than before the war. Hence, if rents were freed from legal control and left to seek their own levels, as much housing as was occupied before the war would be distributed more equally than it was in 1940. That better housing goes under free market conditions to those who have larger incomes or more wealth is, argue Friedman and Stigler, simply a reason for taking long-term measures to reduce the inequality of income and wealth. Better, therefore, to attack directly existing inequalities in income and wealth at their source than to ration each of the hundreds of goods and services that compose people's standard of living:

> It is the height of folly to permit individuals to receive unequal money incomes and then to take elaborate and costly measures to prevent them

31

Housing Shortage

from using their incomes.

(Friedman and Stigler, 1946)

(b) <u>'If rent controls were to be removed, landlords would benefit'</u>

Friedman and Stigler concede that rents would certainly rise, except in the so-called black market, and so would the incomes of landlords. But, they ask, is this a real objection? Some groups will gain under any system of rationing, and it is certainly true that landlords have benefited less than any other large group from wartime expansion. However, the ultimate solution, in Friedman and Stigler's opinion, must come in new construction. Any increase or improvement of housing for such persons depends in large part on the construction of new properties to rent: 'It is an odd way to encourage new rental construction (that is, becoming a landlord) by grudging enterprising builders an attractive return.' (Friedman and Stigler 1946.)

(c) <u>'Under a free market in housing a rise in rents means inflation, or leads to one'</u>

Price inflation is a rise of many individual prices, and Friedman and Stigler contend that it is much easier to attack the threat at its source, which they argue is the increased family income and liquid resources that finance the increased spending on almost everything. In short, heavy taxation, government economies, and the control of the stock of money, are the fundamental weapons to fight inflation.

> Tinkering with millions of individual prices - the rent of a house A in San Francisco, the price of steak B in Chicago, the price of a suit C in New York - means dealing clumsily and ineffectively with the symptoms and results, of inflation instead of the real causes.

(Friedman and Stigler, 1946)

In effect, fiscal and monetary controls are not being invoked, and are not likely to be, by the removal of rent ceilings.

(ii) Rationing by chance and favouritism
Supply effects in cases where legal ceilings are imposed on rents will inevitably lead to a reduction in the number of places to rent. In the United States, Friedman and Stigler point out that money incomes doubled between the beginning and the end of the war and families were able to pay substantially higher rents than before. Yet legally they need pay no more even though they are 'crying' to get more and better housing. Similarly, landlords facing a declining return on their investments as costs rise will sell their properties so adding to the conditions of shortage. Friedman and Stigler cite the advertisements in the San Francisco Chronicle which documented the effect of rent ceilings. In 1906, after the earthquake, when rents were free to rise, there was one 'wanted to rent' for every ten 'houses or apartments for rent'; in 1946, there were 375 'wanted to rent' for every ten 'for rent'.

The demand effects of a situation of rent ceilings is explored later, but one aspect which concerns supply is what happens to existing accommodation under property rationing by chance and favouritism. The main supply effect is a reduction in the efficiency with which housing is used by those who are not forced to double-up in the face of shortage. Incentives to economise space are much weaker in conditions of control, because rents are now lower relative to average money incomes. Moreover, the scarcity resulting from rent ceilings imposes new impediments to the efficient use of housing. A tenant is unlikely to abandon his 'overly-large' apartment to begin a search for accommodation of a more appropriate size. This, of course, feeds back to the demand side in that every time a vacancy does occur the landlord is likely to give preference in renting to smaller families or the single. In short, argue Friedman and Stigler, the removal of rent ceilings would bring about a doubling-up in an entirely different manner. In a free rental market those people would yield up space who considered the sacrifice of space repaid by the rent received. Doubling-up would be by those who had space to spare and wanted extra income, not, as now, by those who act from a sense of family duty or obligation, regardless of space available or other circumstances.

Within the supply effects of rent control, Friedman and Stigler conclude that ceilings cause haphazard and arbitrary allocation of space, inefficient use of space, retardation of new construction and indefinite continuance of rent ceilings (as experienced in the UK) or subsidisation of new construction and a future depression in residential building.

Rydenfelt (1980) has a similar conclusion on the supply effects of control. He argues that, the 'popular opinion' encouraged by defenders of rent control, that the Swedish housing shortage was a product of the war, does not accord with the evidence demonstrated either by data from Stockholm or Malmo. In fact, all of the data indicate that the shortage during the war years was insignificant compared with that after the war. According to Rydenfelt it was only in the post-war rent control era that the housing shortage assumed such proportions that it became Sweden's most serious social problem.

He also provides an explanation of people's thinking as to why shortage emerged, which is as relevant today as ever. The rapidly increasing housing shortage after 1945 soon ripened into a situation which could no longer be attributed to the supply dislocations that were supposedly created by the war. New explanations were needed. That most commonly adopted by the general public was the assumption that the shortage was a consequence of insufficient construction activity. If population increased at a faster rate than the number of housing units there was bound to be a shortage, people thought; and they therefore adopted the untested assumption that construction was lagging behind. In Rydenfelt's view, among the defenders of rent control this population growth explanation became for a long time the most fashionable.

These conclusions of Rydenfelt (1980) are backed up by the forecasts, at the same period in history, of Professor Hechscher[1] who considered that any shortage could not be blamed on insufficient construction activity:

> In a free housing market no shortage would exist at the present rate of construction. On the other hand, no rate of construction activity can eliminate the shortage under the present order. It is like the tub of Danaides, from which water was constantly flowing out at a faster rate than it could be poured in.

Rydenfelt (1980) has also pointed where, in his view, the blame for housing shortage should be laid:

> The cause of the housing shortage is to be found entirely on the demand side. As a consequence of rent control and the relative reduction of the rent - the manipulated low price - demand has increased to such an extent that an ever-widening gap between supply and demand has developed in spite of the high levels of construction activity. Our great mistake is that we always seek the cause of a shortage on the supply side, while it is as frequently to be found on the demand side. The housing shortage will be our companion for ever, unless we prevent demand from running ahead of production.

We do not entirely concur with this conclusion. In a rent control situation, while the supply of housing in total may increase, that available to private tenants will tend to decrease. Landlords will exit the market where possible and new properties will be deterred. This is clear from the British evidence on the supply effects of rent control to which we now turn.

Maclennan (1978) examined the effects of the Rent Act 1974 on the furnished rental housing sector in the city of Glasgow.

35

Housing Shortage

His study, although limited to only one city, is one of the most detailed analyses undertaken. Where possible the efficiency of a housing policy should be assessed in relation to other effects on housing throughout the United Kingdom. As Maclennan himself points out, the absence of official statistics suitable for monitoring the Rent Acts effects precludes such an exercise. Costs of collecting appropriate information on rental sector sales, vacancies and letting procedures inevitably restrict analysis to a particular local housing market.

Maclennan conducts a rigorous analysis of the behaviour of landlords and tenants, before, after and during implementation of the 1974 Rent Act. He found that the letting behaviour of landlords can be interpreted as a desire to continue 'letting, but to reduce the risks of furnished renting'. According to Maclennan:

> Such rational behaviour on the part of landlords does mean that legal landlord behaviour can, in the long run, frustrate one objective of the 1974 Rent Act - that is, to ensure a supply of furnished private lets with full security of tenure for 'poor families' within the sector.

(Maclennan 1978)

Maclennan is unambivalent in his conclusion on the dire supply effects of the 1974 Rent Act:

> The 1974 Rent Act reduced the supply of furnished properties, although this reduction was ameliorated by the ability of landlords to alter their product or tenantry and so escape the restrictions of the Act. If the 1974 Rent Act was intended to discourage private renting further, then it can be said to have been an unequivocal success. However, this view fails to consider the costs and benefits of rental sector decline. The reduction in private rental supply has not, everywhere, been matched by an expansion in

municipal property available to the typically young, transient tenants of the sector. Given the rising price of property which precludes entry into the owner-occupied sector, furnished sector tenants, at least in Glasgow, are trapped between the effects of the Rent Act and intransigent policies on municipal letting.

(Maclennan 1978)

Conclusion

The examples examined in this chapter show clearly that rent control results in a 'shortage' of rental accommodation as a consequence of both supply-side and demand-side effects. On the supply-side there will be a reduction in the total amount of rental housing available and a decline in the efficiency of its use. Rent control will, according to the empirical evidence, also cause an expansion of demand. In some cases - San Francisco in the 1940s and post-war Sweden for example - we observe the perhaps ironic phenomenon of <u>total</u> growth of construction activity meeting or out-pacing population growth while the measured housing shortage is increasing.

Our review of the evidence is, by necessity, incomplete. Many other instances of studies drawing similar conclusions could be cited. The unanimity of the literature on the effects of rental market controls is striking (and worrying). In the next chapter we turn to another effect of controls on rents and evictions - the deterioration of dwelling quality.

Note

1.   In Dagens Nyheter, 15 May 1948.

CHAPTER FOUR

DETERIORATION OF DWELLING QUALITY

In many cases, rent control appears to be the most efficient technique presently known to destroy a city - except for bombing.

Assar Lindbeck

In many - but not all - rent and eviction control situations we expect to observe a deterioration in the quality of dwellings. When only rents are controlled landlords will probably try and eject tenants and sell the property on the free market for owner-occupied dwellings. If this is not possible as a consequence of eviction controls it may be in their interests to reduce or eliminate spending on repairs and maintenance both as a means of 'cutting one's losses' and to act as a stimulus for the tenant to leave.

Often residential tenancies legislation incorporates measures to deal with this eventuality. For example, landlords may be allowed to charge a higher rent if they can satisfy the authorities that they are properly maintaining their properties. In other cases, the legislation has required landlords to maintain dwellings without compensation, while in yet others tenants have been allowed to withhold rent payments to make compulsory repairs.

The incentive facing the landlord with regard to repairs is also influenced by expectations about the future of the controls on the market. If controls are expected to be very long-lasting (and sitting tenants expected to remain in occupancy) the landlord may even allow structural damage to go unattended. However, if controls are thought to be temporary this sort of neglect will not be expected.

In this chapter we review firstly the theoretical link between the nature of the rental market controls and the impact on the quality of rental housing. This extends the analysis sketched in Chapter 2. We then proceed to review the empirical evidence on the quality effects of controls.

The Theory

The effects of rental market controls on the 'quality' of rental housing depends crucially on the nature of the controls and expectations about how long they will last. In many cases the legislation has been changed in response to observed deterioration in the quality of the rental housing stock. Sometimes the law has contained 'carrots' to induce landlords to maintain their properties, while in other cases it has used the 'stick' approach to the problem by punishing landlords in some way. Our analyses in Chapter 2 give some clues of the likely impacts on quality of alternative regulatory regimes.

One obvious element of importance is whether the legislation contains strong 'security of tenure' provisions. Where it does not the landlord has a way out that does not involve allowing repair and maintenance spending to lapse - the tenants can simply be ejected. Where evictions are controlled, this is not possible.

Initially, at least, most systems of rental market control regulate the level of rents irrespective of the quantity of housing services produced by the dwelling. This means that the rent per unit of housing service can be raised by allowing the dwelling to deteriorate in quality.

One reaction of the legislators is to make the rent allowed to be charged dependent on the quantity of housing services rendered by the dwelling. This means that a deterioration in quality will reduce the total rent received while an increase in quality will increase it. This may result in some incentive to maintain the property.

A second means of attaining the maintenance of

dwelling quality is to require landlords to maintain dwellings without any compensation. In some cases, tenants have been allowed to make repairs themselves and withhold rent payments to cover the expenses. While the 'stick' may work as well as the 'carrot', we believe it is unfair to penalise property owners further by imposing requirements on them unless they are compensated. The 'stick' approach also has the unfortunate side-effect of increasing tensions between landlords and tenants.

The Empirical Evidence
It is in regard to the effects of housing quality that the Swedish market socialist economist, Assar Lindbeck, made his famous statement about the effects of ths type of legislation:

> In many cases, rent control appears to be the most efficient technique presently known to destroy a city - except for bombing.

(Lindbeck, 1967)

Rent control, in one form or another, has been present in Sweden for many years. Another Swede, Sven Rydenfelt (1980, pp.55-56) has observed its effects:

> As a result of control and lower rental income, owners' ability to maintain their apartment houses has declined. In particular, their incentive for such upkeep which is motivated by an aesthetic or comfort point of view, has dwindled.

> In a free market there is never a shortage of dwellings and flats to let. If the owner in such a market does not keep his property in good condition he runs the risk of losing his tenants and being left with empty flats and losses in rental income. In a controlled market with severe shortages, the owner is under no such compulsion. No matter how badly maintained is his

41

property, there are always long queues of homeless people willing to rent his shabby, poorly
maintained flats.

Since there is no economic incentive to encourage the owners to repair, even basic upkeep -
which in the long-run is necessary to prevent
serious quality deterioration (i.e. slums) - is
neglected. A development of this kind is difficult
to describe in quantitative terms.

(Rydenfelt, 1980)

Elsewhere in Europe the same phenomenon has been
noted. For example, consider the striking evidence of a
'Parisian plight' provided by de Jouvenel (1948, p.37):

Even a very lenient officialdom estimates that
there are about 16,000 buildings which are in
such a state of disrepair that there is nothing
that can be done but to pull them down. Nor are
the remainder altogether satisfactory. To go into
sordid details, 80 per cent of Parisians have no
bath or shower, more than half must go out of
their lodgings to find a lavatory, and a fifth do
not even have running water in the lodgings.
Little more than one in six of existing buildings
is pronounced satisfactory and in good condition
by the public inspectors. Lack of repair is ruining
even these.

Owners can hardly be blamed. They are not in a
financial position to keep up their buildings, let
alone to improve them. The condition of the
owners can hardly be believed. To take an
example of a very common situation, here is a
lady who owns three buildings containing 34
apartments, all inhabited by middle-class families. Her net loss from the apartments, after
taxes and repairs is $80 a year. Not only must

her son put her up and take care of her, but he must also pay out the $80. She cannot sell; there are no buyers.

When the owner tries to milk a little net income from his property by cutting down the repairs, he runs great risks. Another person postponed repairs on his roofs; rain filtering into an apartment spoiled a couple of armchairs. He was sued for damages and condemned to pay a sum amounting to three years of the tenant's paltry rent.

The miserable condition of owners is easily explained. While rents since 1914 have at the outside multiplied 6.8 times, taxes have grown 13.2 times and the cost of repairs has increased from 120 to 150 times the 1914 price.

(de Jouvenel, 1948)

Precisely the same effect was observed just after the Second World War in Britain. Paish (1952, p.50) noted the situation of landlords caught in a cost-price squeeze from which they received no relief until the late 1950s - and even this was inadequate. According to Paish:

The economic aspects of rent restriction reveal disadvantages at least comparable with those of its legal and equitable aspects. There are mainly two: the impairment of the landlords' ability and incentive to maintain premises in good condition, and the impediments which the Acts place in the way of mobility of labour.

As regards the first of these, it is common ground that the cost of maintaining and repairing houses has risen markedly since before the war, probably more than twice everywhere, and in some areas three times or more. At these prices,

Deterioration of Dwelling Quality

many landlords are unable to pay for adequate repairs out of the controlled rents and leave themselves any income at all, while others, especially owners of the older property unsuitable for owner-occupancy, find that it pays them better to collect what income they can until their property becomes actually uninhabitable than to spend money on repairs which will never yield a reasonable return on the expenditure. The probability that property will be treated in this way is increased by the tendency of the better landlords, faced with the choice between running their property at a loss and allowing it to decay, to sell it for what it will fetch to those who are less scrupulous in their methods of management. Thus, much property is being allowed to degenerate into slums, or at best maintained at a level much below that which is economically desirable and which it would have paid landlords to achieve if rents had been allowed to find their market level. For the ultimate results of this policy we have only to look across the English Channel ...

(Paish, 1952)

Even the 'New World' has not been immune from the effects of rental market controls creating slums. The Institute of Public Affairs in Australia (1954, p.124) blamed rent control for the deterioration of the dwelling stock in the inner suburbs of Melbourne:

Rents have lagged so many laps behind costs that few landlords are able to make repairs or improvements to their properties. The cost of this type of work has risen much more than other costs because of the dearth of skilled tradesmen and materials. Many tenanted houses and business premises are falling into disrepair for lack of proper maintenance. Whether driving

44

down the main shopping block or side residential streets, in most of the older suburbs of Melbourne one is met with a picture of almost unrelieved dinginess and dilapidation. Government attention is concentrated on the erection of new housing, oblivious to the fact that the stock of old houses is being hastened to premature decay through rent control.

(The Institute of Public Affairs, Australia, 1954)

Conclusion
The above instances, again, represent only a sample of the observations made about the effects of rent control on quality. Perhaps de Jouvenel (1948) exposes, better than most, the road to ruin from rent control:

Possibly the French example may prove of some interest and use to our friends across the sea. It goes to show that rent control is self-perpetuating and culminates in both the physical ruin of housing and the legal dispossession of the owners. It is enough to visit the houses in Paris to reach conclusions. The havoc wrought here is not the work of the enemy but of our own measures.

(de Jouvenel, 1948)

Without exception, the verdict is hostile to rent control. Each of the authors cited in this chapter points to the adverse effects on housing quality of control.

While controls may be popular and beneficial to existing tenants, they restrict resource allocation in rental markets like any other price controls. With rents fixed below the market clearing price, effective demand exceeds the supply of accommodation for rent. The supply effects of rent control may be summarised as helping to create and perpetuate economic shortage of rented housing, fostering the dilapidation of housing, and deterring new lettings and new construction.

45

CHAPTER FIVE

EXCESS DEMAND AND ITS CONSEQUENCES

...the use of higher rents to ration housing has been made illegal by the imposition of rent ceilings, and the rationing is by chance and favouritism.

Milton Friedman and George Stigler

In Chapters 3 and 4, we reviewed the international evidence of the effects of rental controls on the quantity of rental housing available and its quality. As anticipated in our theoretical analysis in Chapter 2, the effects are very clear indeed. The quantity of both existing and new private rental housing made available decreases, sometimes very rapidly, and the quality of the remaining rental housing tends to deteriorate more rapidly than it would otherwise.

This chapter chronicles the international verdict on another set of effects expected from rental market controls. The effects of rent control should, as noted in Chapter 3, show up on both the supply and demand side of the market. Low rents would be expected to not only lead to a reduction in supply, but also to an increase in demand. That is, rent ceilings result in a situation of 'excess demand'. The theoretical expectation of this was shown clearly in Chapter 2.

Excess demand, in turn, manifests itself in two major ways. Firstly, where price cannot act as a rationing device, sellers will tend to use other criteria in 'discriminating' between potential tenants. Secondly, excess demand is such that willingness-to-pay for the available quantity is greater than the controlled price, and this encourages 'black market' activities. Both of these repercussions of rental market controls have been observed in many instances where this type of legislation has been introduced. We each consider each in turn.

We also take the opportunity in this chapter to examine another set of practices that arise in controlled rental markets. In such situations landlords often have an incentive to get rid of tenants even if they are 'good tenants' - the property is worth more without them than with. Often rather unpleasant methods have been used in ejecting tenants.

Non-Price Competition

In a world where many people are prone to discriminate against or for others on the basis of attributes such as race, religion, etc., it seems to us unfortunate to introduce or retain legislation which encourages this type of activity. Rental market control is an example of the type of legislation which has this effect.

In a free market situation rent is the device which rations the available supply of housing. While a landlord may require different rent levels to accept different types of tenants and, indeed, may set very high rents to deter those he does not want, the ability to offer a higher rent is a means of overcoming 'disabilities'. A person with a disadvantage can offer a higher rent in an attempt to secure a tenancy. If the landlord does not accept it is either because the extra rent does not cover the anticipated extra costs of that tenant or that he is willing to bear the cost of his prejudices. The more competitive is the market the most costly these prejudices can be.

Perhaps the clearest concise statement of the issue of discrimination in a free market is in Milton Friedman's Capitalism and Freedom (1962, Chapter 7). There it is noted that the businessman who expresses preferences in his business dealings is 'at a disadvantage compared to other individuals who do not. Such an individual is in effect imposing higher costs on himself than are other

48

individuals who ... in a free market ... will tend to drive
him out' (pp. 110-111). In other words, a free market is a
device for limiting the degree of discrimination by bringing home its costs to the person practising it.

Not so in a price-controlled market. Because of
excess demand as a consequence of rent control, the
landlord will have numerous applicants for any available
property coming onto the market. Suppose the landlord is
a Christian with strong moral views and has to choose
between a God-fearing married couple and a pair of
homosexuals. It is unlikely that the latter will, under the
rent control, get the tenancy even though they may be
willing to pay more for it than the successful applicants.
There is, under rent control, no cost to the landlord in
'discriminating' according to his likes and dislikes. Minor-
ities of all kinds - religious, sexual, ethnic, etc. - will tend
to be the losers under these circumstances.

Often rental market controls include provisions
making various types of discrimination illegal. For this
reason it is difficult to get evidence on the extent of this
invidious practice. Nonetheless we were able to find two
examples of where non-price rationing has been observed.

The first of these is the case of San Francisco as
observed by Friedman and Stigler, where 'chance and
favouritism' was the rationing procedure.

> Rental property is now rationed by various forms
> of chance and favouritism. First priority goes to
> the family that rented before the housing
> shortage and is willing to remain in the same
> dwelling.
>
> Second priority goes to two classes among recent
> arrivals:
> (i) persons willing and able to avoid or evade rent
> ceilings, either by some legal device or by paying
> a cash supplement to the OPA ceiling rent;
> (ii) friends or relatives of landlords or other
> persons in charge of renting dwellings.

Excess Demand and its Consequences

> Last priority is likely to go to the man who must work to support his family and whose wife must care for small children. He and his wife can spend little time looking for the needle in the haystack. And if he should find a place it may well be refused him because a family with small children is less desirable as tenants than a childless family.

(Friedman and Stigler, 1946)

Note that this quotation makes reference to black market dealings, the subject matter of the next section.

Our second example is from Canberra, Australia, where in a more recent instance of rental market control in the mid 1970s, it was found that groups of young people wishing to occupy a family house were not favoured. So much so was the problem that, according to the Real Estate and Stock Institute of Australia (1975, p.166):

> The rent controls will virtually eliminate accommodation for groups unless there is recognition by the authorities that a higher risk is involved for the landlord.

(Real Estate and Stock Institute of Australia, 1975)

Black Market Dealings

The second major consequence of price ceilings is the encouragement to the abuse of the law through black market dealings. We feel that it is undesirable to bring the law into disrepute by encouraging law breaking - but this is precisely what price controls do. The imposition of price ceilings create an interest for both parties - the seller and the buyer - to break the law. Consider the simple demand and supply model of Figure 5.1.

Suppose that price is initially at P_0 and quantity Q_0 in a free market situation. When a price ceiling of P_1 is imposed, sellers reduce the amount they are willing to offer to Q_1. While sellers are legally bound to charge only P_1 per unit for this amount, buyers are willing to pay P^D. Because P^D exceeds P_1, buyers are prepared to pay more than the actual price to secure more of the good - paying more to get more is in their interests because they value incremental units at more than P_1. On the other hand sellers are willing to supply more if they can get above P_1. In short, both parties have a pecuniary interest in breaking the law (i.e. trading at a price above P_1) which is, in this sense, a 'crime without victim'.

Figure 5.1

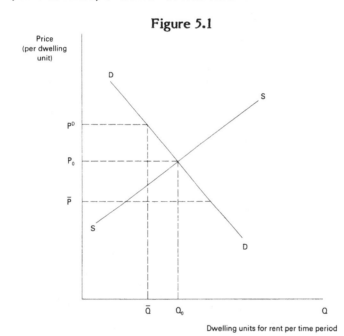

Where supply is for some reason fixed there will be a 'victim' from black market trading. The honest individual who does not break the law will tend to miss out in these circumstances - the sharp operators will procure supplies at the expense of the meek, even if the latter are prepared to pay more than the control price.

Excess Demand and its Consequences

Because of its illegality it is difficult to get evidence on the black market. Occasional indications arise. We have already seen Friedman and Stigler's claim that above-rent payments were made in San Francisco. Cheung (1980, pp.25-26) refers to the situation in Hong Kong during the 1920s.

The payment of 'shoe money' had been a tradition in Hong Hong long before the ordinance was ever considered. Legend attributes the phrase to a polite euphemism for payments to middlemen who had to 'wear out their shoes' in searching out living quarters for clients. By extension, the term can be applied to 'courtesy' payments direct to landlords by prospective tenants trying to gain tenancy. Not infrequently in crowded post-war Hong Kong such payments might amount to several hundred times the monthly rental.

To discourage this type of evasion, the ordinance explicitly prohibited side payments to the landlord or demands by the landlord 'of any sum whatsoever, in addition to the (standard) rent'. Since voluntary gifts by the lessee could not be totally forestalled, the real thrust of the regulation was against exactions by the landlord who for infractions faced a threat of court action and a fine up to one thousand dollars. To clarify the matter, the Attorney General explained that the Council considered it unnecessary to prohibit the traditional fee for 'searching' since 'while the Bill remains in operation there is no reason why anyone should be forced to pay any excessive 'shoe money' ... if (he) pays the standard rent ... as long as the Bill remains in force, (he) cannot be turned out'.

The reasoning was partially correct. The end point, however, was the question of the right of possession. If for any cause whatever the land-lord could give weight to his threat of eviction, the tenant would have incentive to offer voluntary side payment. When standard rent is lower than market rent, both the resident tenant and the prospective tenant will have reason to offer a lump sum rather than forego a lease. Such a side payment can effectively be prohibited only if a tenant is in residence and the landlord has no right to evict him.

(Cheung, 1980)

Means of Getting Vacant Possession

Where properties can be re-let at a market rent (as is often the case) or sold in the uncontrolled market for owner-occupancy (which is always the case), landlords subject to severe restrictions on evictions may turn to other ways of removing tenants - some legal and others definitely not.

Most rental market legislation is very complex, the result of years of amendments which try to plug holes or give relief as a consequence of pressures built-up by earlier measures. The opaqueness is often further heightened by the fact that these amendments are built upon a piece of legislation dating back to feudal times. Naturally, this provides considerable opportunities for the legal profession to find and exploit loopholes in the legislation on behalf of landlords. One Australian legal practitioner became an expert on the New South Wales Landlord and Tenant Act in the late 1950s and early 1960s and reputedly made a fortune in evicting tenants. Disbarred as a result of these activities, Peter Clyne later wrote a book on the legislation (see Clyne, 1970) and developed a career in the tax avoidance industry.

Where legal efforts fail, rather unpleasant methods have been resorted to in ejecting tenants. We have heard of cases involving threats of and actual violence, intimidation through late night 'anonymous' phone calls

53

Excess Demand and its Consequences

and other types of annoying behaviour. One Sydney landlord offered to paint the house one weekend while the tenants were away. Upon their return they found the house had indeed been painted - the interior, including doors and windows, was jet black.[1] Webster (1980, p.174) has told us of a practice in Sydney during the 1950s where one group of tenants would take over neighbouring properties (which were presumably worthless in their presence):

> A family would pay 'key money' to get the tenancy of a terrace or semi-detached house. Three or four families, with children, would then move in. They would harass the neighbours with brawls, late parties, acts of indecency, trucks and cars parked in gateways, and even threats and insults to the women-folk when they met them on the street with no witnesses. Soon the neighbours would leave in disgust. The group would take over the vacated flat and set to work on the next. An effective display of the 'domino theory'.

(Webster, 1980)

The situation in Hong Kong in the 1920s provides another example of the extent to which people will go in order to eject tenants from a controlled property. According to Cheung (1980, p.27):

> Great was the frustration of landlords, in a period when free-market rents were soaring and population pressures expanding. Some tried such ruses as intentionally making their properties undesirable to tenants. A bare three months after the imposition of the ordinance it was reported that 'certain landlords have gone so far as to remove windows in wet weather and even staircases to drive the tenants out'. Penalties for such antics were promptly inserted in the

ordinance, and by June 1922 the loopholes had been plugged up by the new provision.

Almost the sole remedy now remaining for the landlord who hoped to obtain free-market rents was the drastic one of demolishing and re-building his property. This prospect was brightened to some extent by the fact that the existing ordinance required no compensation to be paid to tenants thus evicted.

(Cheung, 1980)

A Final Point
We know that rental housing markets, even when completely free, are not always the scenes of great harmony between landlords and tenants. A lot is at stake in the tenancy contract, there is plenty of room for conflict and there is still some of that old 'feudal' animosity around. Problems must be expected to occur even if the authorities take a laissez-faire attitude except in regard to protecting the voluntarily-entered contractual rights of individuals.

However, we also believe very strongly that the existence of controls on the market lead to the development of a new set of tensions considerably worse than those in a free market - discrimination is enhanced, illegal dealings are encouraged and drastic measures to escape the controls are often resorted to. Speaking as concerned citizens we find these effects most disturbing because they reinforce what we see as a general breakdown in social cohesion and the respect of the legal system. This most unfortunate process does not need any additional impetus.

Note

1. This case and others are chronicled in the New South Wales Royal Commission report (see Parliament of New South Wales, 1961).

CHAPTER SIX

LABOUR IMMOBILITY

> *... private rented housing ... has almost disappeared in Britain and ... cries out for revival in the name of labour mobility (and thus more jobs).*

The Economist, 3.1.1987

There is an old saying - 'When you're on a good thing stick to it'. The occupant of a subsidised house or flat is in the position of receiving a benefit from that tenancy. This in itself is not a cause of immobility. However, when combined with the scarcity of alternative accommodation at a comparable rent level, this can be a problem. Certainly, in the case of Britain the policies towards housing have tended to hamper the correction of a marked structural imbalance between the north and the south. Further, within areas there is a disincentive for people to adjust their housing consumption to changed circumstances. Both of these effects could be the basis of very large costs to society as a whole.

Internationally the effects of rental market control on both labour mobility and the fostering of the inefficient use of house-space, have often been observed. This chapter reviews the evidence on these effects from around the world and, as usual, finds a strong degree of unanimity about the observations. Because of its great importance in Britain, we dwell in particular on the issue of labour immobility and review some recent estimates of the adverse efficiency effects of immobilising housing policies in Britian.

Inefficient Use of House Space
Sitting tenants in both privately rented and council houses tend to sit, even if their circumstances change such that they would prefer either more or less space than that provided by their present abode. Over time the situation becomes steadily worse as circumstances alter and as new tenants take what they can get rather than what they may like. It is only when the inconvenience is so great that the tenant will move voluntarily, in spite of the inability to find another controlled dwelling, that the house space is freed, hopefully for a more suited tenant.

The sort of changes in circumstances that occur are things like the family growing-up and leaving home; increases in the family size when children are born; the desire to take in a relative; the death of a family member; changes in income, etc. Over time requirements are changing but the degree of adjustment to them under rent control is less than it would be otherwise.

Apart from the manifest inequities where large families are crammed into small flats while Darby and Joan rattle around in a large house, the use of house space becomes increasingly inefficient. It is unlikely that the tenant values the difference between market rent and regulated rent at the actual amount of the difference. The tenant would probably prefer to have the difference as a lump-sum and be free to choose his own accommodation. As times goes by, the tenant's subjective valuation of the rent differential will tend to decline. That is, the degree of inefficiency of the use of house space becomes greater, relative to that that would occur in a free market.

Schemes that allow tenants to keep the difference between market and controlled rent for a limited period, irrespective of where the tenant lives, help overcome this particular problem while facilitating the ultimate end of rental market control. We discuss them in detail in Chapter 10. For now we finish off our discussion with one observation of the situation created by rental market control in post-war Australia (Bank of New South Wales, 1953, p.129).

> Despite these steps towards more liberal admini-stration the continued existence of rent control has created extremely rigid conditions in the letting of houses. Persons who have a house rented continuously since before the war may still be paying the same rental, though they go in fear of being 'fair rented', but they would be unwilling to move to another area because of the extreme difficulty in securing tenancy of another house. For this reason older people whose children have left the family home may be occupying a house substantially larger than their present needs or desires, and may in fact pay a lower rental than they would for a new but much smaller house. In these circumstances, too, they have a positive financial discouragement from building a new house for themselves at current high costs while they are enjoying a relatively low rental. Few newcomers to the housing market, ex-servicemen, newly married persons, or growing families, have been able to obtain a pre-war rent-controlled dwelling; others have the difficult choice of living with parents, buying a high-cost, post-war home, if they can finance it, paying high rentals for inadequate temporary accommodation or waiting indefinitely for a State-built house ...

(Bank of New South Wales, 1953)

Disincentives to Job Searching

Perhaps even more than the inefficiency through the rigid use of house space is the cost to society caused by the disincentive for people in controlled dwellings to move in search of better job opportunities. This immobility has two adverse effects on efficiency. Firstly, it leads to

Labour Immobility

greater mis-matching of workers to jobs as people forgo opportunities for better jobs, more suited to them, because of the existence of a stationary housing subsidy. Secondly, some workers will be unemployed and will remain idle in spite of job opportunities elsewhere. The difference between their wage and the value they place on leisure activities is a loss to society as a whole.

This lack of mobility has been noted often by experts who have studied the effects of rental market controls. Consider, for example, the observations of the Nobel Prize winning economist, F.A. Hayek, in his 1930 study of rent restrictions in Vienna, (1930, pp.7-9):

> The restrictions on the mobility of manpower caused by rent controls means not only that available accommodation is badly used to satisfy diverse housing requirements. They also have implications for the deployment and recruitment of labour to which too little attention is paid.

> In normal times regional switches in industrial manpower requirements entail considerable labour migration and, despite the unusually large changes in industry in the past decade, migrations have been blocked by rent controls. Left to iself, and given an unfettered wage-structure, this immobility would prevent wages in different regions from evening themselves out, and cause marked variations between the regions.

> As things stand, however, collectively-negotiated wage settlements largely rule out such variations, and two other results therefore follow. First, the wage-earner will choose to commute rather than move whenever his new place of work is within reach of his home, either on a daily or weekly basis, even though he may find this mode of living by no means satisfactory.

The wage-earner who is prevented from moving will have to spend extra time and money, which represent a cut in pay, further aggravated because regional differences have been eliminated. From the economic standpoint, this and all other expenditures incurred by people because they are 'wedded' to their homes are downright wasteful. B. Kautsky points out that the cause of Vienna's increased tram traffic, which doubled between 1913 and 1928 at a time of diminishing population, can only have been this inhibited mobility. P. Vas, admittedly with some exaggeration, estimates that 'the additional fares squeezed out of the Viennese public by rent control alone amounted to at least two-thirds of the annual outlay on new building in the city.

Commuting, however, is not always a feasible alternative to moving house, and if it is not, the result is unemployment. Joseph Schumpeter, writing in Deutsche Volskwirt, once gave a forceful expression to the importance of the correlation between lack of mobility of labour and unemployment, an importance which cannot be rated too highly. I shall merely mention one example of it which came to my notice recently.

A manufacturer of my acquaintance with a factory in a small town some five hours from Vienna and an office in Vienna itself went to the labour exchange in Vienna to ask for an electrical fitter for his provincial factory. Twenty or so fitters, some of whom had been out of work for a long time, applied for the vacancy, but every one of them withdrew rather than give up a protected tenancy in Vienna for unprotected works accommodation. Weeks later the industrialist had still not found his fitter. Every manufacturer in Austria with a factory outside the main industrial centres can tell you countless

61

Labour Immobility

similar stories.

(Hayek, 1930)

Our next observation, from F.W. Paish (1952, p.51), is of Britain in the early post-war period, and draws attention not only to the deleterious effects of rental market controls on labour mobility, but also to the effects on the efficiency of the use of house space, the importance of 'special favour' in procuring a tenancy, and the existence of above-rent payments:

> The second of the economic disadvantages of rent restriction, at least in the short run, is probably even more serious than the first. Rent restriction involves what is in effect a tax on the landlord and a subsidy to the tenant. But it is a subsidy which the tenant receives only so long as he stays in his existing house. Should he leave it for any reason, he is deprived, not only of his subsidy, but also of his right to rent another house even at the full market price. If he happens to live in a council house it may be possible for him, by arrangement with the local authority, to exchange houses with someone else in the same district, or even to be allotted a new house on surrendering his old one. But if he lives in a privately-owned house, or if he wishes to move outside his district, his chance of renting another within a reasonable time is small unless he either has access to some special favour or is prepared to break the law by offering some consideration in addition to the controlled rent. Otherwise, he will have to make do with furnished lodgings until first he qualifies to be regarded as a resident and then his name has slowly climbed to the top of the local authority's housing list. It is little wonder that the much-needed increase in the mobility of labour is so

difficult to achieve.

(Paish, 1952)

Rent control in Israel during the Second World War resulted, by the 1950s, in large disparities between legal and market rents. As reported by Shreiber and Tabriztchi (1976), a practice developed where sitting tenants would introduce a new tenant to the landlord if they wished to leave. The new tenant would pay 'key money' which was shared between the departing tenant (two thirds) and the landlord. This practice was initially illegal but became so widespread that it was legalised in 1958. While we are not suggesting the adoption of this practice in Britain, it is worth noting that it does enhance the degree of mobility in a rent control situation and does provide some relief to the landlord.

More recently in Britain, the existence of a 'north' and 'south' division of the nation has emerged as an enormous problem. The decline of the old industries in the north of England and Scotland have been offset to some extent by the development of new industries in the south. However, while there is an excess demand for labour in the south, this is not being met from the ranks of the unemployed in the north. Housing policies are partly to blame for the continuation of this imbalance.

Rental market controls are causes of immobility for the reasons we have mentioned - people are unwilling to move from a controlled house or flat and cannot find accommodation in the areas where there is work. Council housing subsidies are also very important as an impediment to mobility. Other policies relating to housing, discussed more fully in Chapter 8, have less obvious but more generally immobilising influences on the rental housing market.

The costs of labour immobility are, for an immobilised worker in employment, the difference between the worker's actual wage and that which could be earned in the best possible alternative occupation and, for the unemployed immobilised worker, the difference between

Labour Immobility

the best wage possible and the value placed on leisure by the person. The aggregate cost of immobility would be the total of these differences over all persons concerned. While we do not have an estimate of the cost expressed in this way, we do have an estimate of the immobility cost conceived differently.

Minford, Ashton and Peel (1986) estimate the effects of all major housing market distortions - the Rent Act, subsidised council rents, tax-deductibility of mortgage interest and environmental planning - on the overall level of unemployment. They find that if the rental market were decontrolled and council house rents raised to free market levels, the level of unemployment would have fallen by about 2 percentage points. This is quite a significant result which would entail an increase in gross domestic product of the unskilled wage rate times the increase in employment. This could be about £3,500 million (i.e. 500,000 x £7,000) in 1987 values. This figure does not represent the gain to society - because it ignores the leisure forgone by the newly-employed, it is an over-estimate; and because it omits the gain from a better matching of the presently employed with jobs, it is an underestimate. There would also be a significant gain from the more efficient use of the nation's stock of housing.

A Final Point
Again we feel inclined to take off our hats as positive economic analysts and to make some comments about the costs of rental market controls in a broader context. We have, in this and the previous three chapters, reviewed the international evidence on the effect of regulations of evictions and rents.

These effects are many - reductions in the quantity and quality of the rental housing stock; the stimulus to various 'sharp', illegal and unpleasant practices; and the cementing effects on the movement of people.

It would seem that a succession of governments in various places have been intent on establishing some of the effects of a collectivist economy in a microcosm.

Apart from the manifest economic costs of rental market controls, it must not be forgotten that they involve a severe undermining of private property rights and an interference in the making of contracts. That is, rental market controls are a move towards collectivism. The rights to the income from and to make decisions about the use of private property are compulsorily reduced. The tenant develops an 'interest' in the property without the landlord's consent. The property is, to some extent, removed from the landlord's control to the benefit of others. This is inconsistent with the basis of a free democractic society.

Britain, unlike most other countries, still has a collectivist enclave in the rental housing 'market'. This has, and continues to, involve significant economic costs and much human suffering for very little benefit. As we argue in later chapters, the benefits that do flow from rental market controls can be much better directed to those in need and provided at much lower cost by other means. It is to these questions of policy that we turn in the next four chapters.

CHAPTER SEVEN

HISTORY OF UK RENT CONTROL UNTIL 1979

The decline in importance of the private rented sector ... in the 20th century has been spectacular.

Martin Ricketts

The private rented sector is practically unique in having so much complex legislation formulated and implemented by successive governments on the basis of either political dogma and/or unsubstantiated conventional wisdom.

Ironically, the increase in size and complexity of the recent Rent Acts has been inversely related to the size of the privately rented housing sector. Despite an evident demand for rented accommodation, the rented sector has declined from 45 per cent of the total housing stock in 1945 to 20 per cent in 1970, 13 per cent in 1980, and to less than 10 per cent at the end of 1986.

Some reasons can be advanced to explain this decline. For instance, public aspirations, rising real incomes and the growth of building societies have undoubtedly attracted many tenants out of the private rented sector into owner occupation.

Moreover, there has been 'unfair' local authority competition in the provision of rented housing, with only the excess demand in this sector spilling over into the private rented sector. Further contributing factors might also include taxation policy in respect of both landlord and tenant, redevelopment programmes, and the tremendous political uncertainty over how future governments may legislate for this sector.

Both Conservative and Labour governments would claim to have sought to arrest the decline of private rented accommodation, but their respective utterances have been poorly translated into policy prescriptions.

A Brief History

The continuing decline and future of the privately rented housing sector in the United Kingdom has been the most consistently politicised aspect of housing policy.

Since rent controls were first introduced in the First World War as an emergency measure to prevent war 'profiteering' by landlords in areas where housing shortages emerged as a result of labour inflows for war production, they have been a permanent part of housing policy. In spite of the Housing Acts of 1923, 1925, 1927, 1933 and 1938 which had elements of decontrol, four million houses were still subject to control in 1939, and rent control has remained in one form or another since its original introduction. However, it was only since the 1950s that it has been considered a part of permanent housing policy.

In 1945, the Labour Government considered rent control an appropriate temporary post-war expedient and rents were broadly frozen at 1939 levels. In the Housing (Repairs and Rent) Act of 1954 landlords were permitted to raise rents by a certain amount if repairs to the property had been undertaken but the real problem was the maintenance of rents at 1939 levels in a period of sustained price rises leading to the under-maintenance of property and rigidity within the controlled market.

In the post-war period Conservatives argued that legislation to promote decontrol was a necessary return to normality and market forces after the wartime shortages while Labour considered such wholesale decontrol hastily conceived and based on dubious assumptions. However, it was not until the Rent Act 1957, that an element of decontrol was finally permitted. This Act provided for rent increases for some 5 million controlled tenancies and block decontrol of properties with high rateable values and those properties falling vacant and re-let. Both this Act and its intentions were short lived, for many of the original provisions were never actually implemented and no further measures of decontrol enacted. Greve (1965) has argued that in any case very little was known about the housing situation in England in 1957 and even less known about those who owned and managed some five million dwellings in England in the year the Rent Act became law and in whose houses about 40 per cent of the population lived.

The most important post-war legislation measure has been the Rent Act 1965 which provided both the basic and permanent framework for the present control of rents with the introduction of a formal rent regulation procedure applied to most of the properties decontrolled in 1957. The 1965 Act embodied the notion of 'fair rents', new security of tenure provisions, and a statutory control system for future regulation of rents.

Since 1965, rent control measures have been progressively extended and following the introduction of the Rent Act 1974, nearly all permanently rented private dwellings are now subject to rent regulation and security of tenure provisions.

Under the 1974 Act, rent registration and full security of tenure provisions were extended to the previously relatively uncontrolled 'furnished' sector. Certain exemptions were extended to several classes of landlord, for instances those providing 'board' or those letting their property through a recognised education body. A new legal class of landlord - resident landlord - was defined and exempted from the provisions of the 1974 Act.

Upon the election of a Conservative Government in 1979, the Housing Act 1980 provided for the introduction of short-term tenancies, under which landlord and tenant could agree the terms of the lease and thus the normally very restrictive security of tenure term could be overcome. Any letting, however, under the arrangement for a 'shorthold tenancy' had to be subject to the 'fair rent' provision. Although this measure was intended to deter further furnished sales, it has had little effect to this day as the sector continues to decline. To compete with the other tenure sectors effectively, it was clear during the early 1980s that a new system for regulation or registration of tenancies would be necessary, possibly involving a move by the Government towards decontrol.

The Present Legislative Framework

The Rent Act of 1965 was a major influence on the form of supply of rented accommodation between 1965 and 1974 for it created two separate markets for privately let accommodation as a result of the vital legal distinction between unfurnished and furnished housings. Lettings by private landlords of unfurnished dwellings with a rateable value at the time not exceeding £400 in Greater London and £200 elsewhere were to become regulated tenancies and subject to 'fair rent' registration and security of tenure. This security of tenure provided for a regulated tenancy to be transferred twice to members of a tenant's family at his death. The 'fair rent' was to be determined by Rent Officers and, if subject to appeal, determined by a local Rent Assessment Committee. In fact, the 1965 Rent Act distinguished three separate categories of rent accommodation - the regulated unfurnished market, the unregulated furnished market, and the old controlled housing - which was to be gradually phased into the new regulated sector.

Criteria for a 'Fair Rent'

The determining criteria laid down for the assessment of a 'fair rent' were of critical consequence for rental housing:

(a)   In determining for the purpose of this Act what rent is or would be a fair rent under a regulated tenancy of a dwelling house, regard shall be had, subject to the following provisions of this section, to all circumstances (other than personal circumstances) and in particular to the age, character and locality of the dwelling house and to its state of repair.

(b)   For the purpose of the determination it shall be assumed that the number of persons seeking to become tenants of similar dwelling houses in the locality which are available for letting on such terms.

Under (a), a 'fair' rent is determined by reference to the attributes of the property and not the financial or personal circumstances of the tenant. Indeed, the ability of the existing tenant to pay his rent, i.e. his personal circumstances, is specifically excluded from consideration. Under (b), the scarcity value of the accommodation is to be ignored. In other words, for the purposes of valuation, the number of dwellings in the locality is assumed to be equal to the number of tenants seeking accommodation irrespective of what they are prepared to pay. The intention would appear to be that only 'abnormal' scarcity should be ignored and the rent set at a level where all 'need' is met. In the context of a perfectly competitive market, absence of such 'scarcity' would be achieved in the long run at the equilibrium level. However, the implication of the above interpretation is that, unless long-run equilibrium assuming a perfectly competitive market is already achieved, the 'fair rent' is permanently below the market clearing rent and conditions are created whereby there is no incentive for landlords to increase the supply of accommodation. These aspects need some clarification.

An Economic Interpretation of a 'Fair Rent'
While the notion of a 'fair rent' is an evident central component of UK housing policy, its theoretical derivation and relationship to economic forces is obscure. A model developed by Cooper and Stafford (1980) attempts one interpretation of a 'fair rent'.

Clearly any economic interpretation is fraught with difficulties for the legal definition provides considerable scope for highly subjective interpretations.

History of UK Rent Control until 1979

The model represented in Figure 7.1, embraces the following assumptions:

(a) Housing units are homogeneous with the same site value and each family can only possess one dwelling unit.

(b) OS_1 is the actual stock of housing to rent and S_1S_1 is a perfectly inelastic short-run supply curve.

(c) S_2S_2 is the long-run supply curve assuming a perfectly competitive market with all firms having the same long-run minimum average costs and no technological or pecuniary externalities.

Figure 7.1

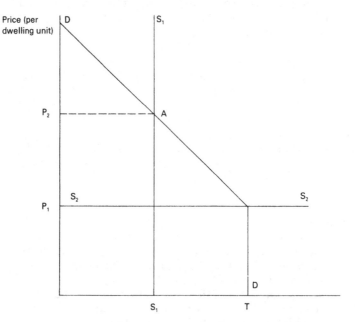

In a perfectly competitive market, P_1 is the 'fair rent' because it would be the rent in the absence of scarcity under constant cost conditions, i.e. the long run perfectly competitive equilibrium rent level. Thus P_1, the 'fair rent', is defined as the level where, in the absence of abnormal circumstances, need would be equated to supply with neither the landlord nor the tenant penalised. Under this determination of the 'fair rent', the government assumes that OT families are both ready and able (at least with assistance through rent allowances) to pay a rent of P_1 for some standard of accommodation of given quality and location. In this context, the rent of P_1 is fair to both landlords and tenants and the demand curve DD will, under these assumptions, have a kink which will coincide with the 'fair rent' P_1. Demand is therefore perfectly inelastic up to and including the fair rent level on the earlier assumption that people are only able to possess one dwelling unit and are not able to respond to low prices by demanding to rent more than one unit.

An initial situation of disequilibrium is assumed in the model with P_1 rent prevailing as the 'fair rent'. While OT families are ready and willing to pay P_1, supply in the short run is only OS_1. Therefore, in the short run at least, equilibrium can only be achieved at a rent of P_2. In the long run, assuming a perfectly competitive market, new entrants would ensure that a rent of P_1 would ultimately be attained and OT families housed.

In Figure 7.2, the more realistic assumption that long-run supply is subject to increasing costs is made and the supply curve S_2S_2 slopes upwards from left to right. Since no obvious long-run solution presents itself, given the control of rent at P_1, the state is faced with a number of possibilities but they all pose difficulties.

Having examined economic models of the effects of rent control, some consideration should now be given to the objectives of government and their compatibility with predictions of the models, albeit taking account of their very restrictive assumptions.

Policies Since the Rent Act, 1965

At the time of the implementation of the Rent Act 1965, the Report of the Committee on Housing in Greater London (the Milner Holland Report) concluded that an acute shortage of rented housing existed in London resulting in extensive multiple occupation, overcrowding and lack of domestic facilities, due not to unreasonable or excessive rents, but to the relationship between tenants' income and rent level. In short, the Committee considered that it was not rent control, per se, which had prompted the reduction of privately rented accommodation in London, but the political and economic climate facing landlords and the very slow upward adjustment of rents in line with rising incomes and costs. In comparison with other capital cities abroad, London's proportion of rented accommodation was low, but other countries' legislation permitted frequent rent adjustment by reference to appropriate price indices together with a body of code to protect and secure tenants in their accommodation. Unlike other European cities, virtually no new housing had been built for private rental since before the Second World War. The Milner Holland Report attributed the demise and problems in the private sector to the absence of government loans or subsidies in Britain compared with other European governments and to the effects of government emphasis on council housing and the assistance to owner-occupiers through tax-reliefs as an accidental outcome of the fiscal system. In effect, local authority housing had proved too competitive for the private rented sector to survive and thus its complementary role was grossly undermined. Only by realistic rent regulation, argued the Committee, could landlords operate in a conducive climate which would not induce the neglect of property or force landlords out of business. This requirement led to the Committee's wholesale condemnation of rent controls as they had been applied in Britain over the past fifty years on the grounds that they persisted in hiding the real cost of supplying and maintaining accommodation, and perpetuated and increased stress rather than offering any relief as intended. In the Report, a

74

comparison was made between the average weekly cost at that time of a dwelling, including land, of £5,500, under various types of tenure. While a local authority could set the weekly rent of £3.40, a housing association operating at cost rent would have to charge £7.70, a private landlord £10.10 and an owner-occupier, after tax relief, would pay £6.35. Although the Committee did not go into precise detail of the calculations behind these illustrative figures, these differences were intended to explain lack of landlord investment and even further to delineate the separate sub-markets for housing and the emanating imperfections as a result of quite different fiscal and legislative controls in each housing sub-market.

Figure 7.2

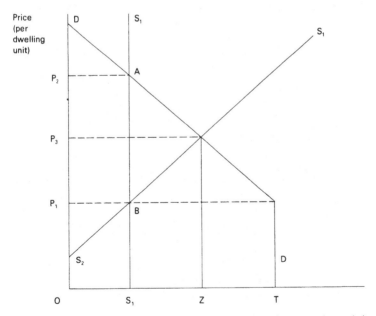

History of UK Rent Control until 1979

Following the consolidation of the Rent Act 1965 in the Rent Act of 1968, the Government set up the Committee on the Rent Acts (Francis Committee), which was to report on the workings of the Rent Act 1968 and the relationship between the codes governing furnished and unfurnished lettings. Unfortunately, the Committee's terms of reference did not extend to examination of the concept of a fair rent and critical appraisal of the factors determining it. In the very brief reference to the operation of rent regulation the majority Report felt that the rent regulation procedure worked well and even tentatively proposed a long-term merger between unfurnished and furnished accommodation. While a minority Report recommended that all furnished accommodation should be brought within the regulated tenancies and granted full security of tenure, the majority Report came out against early extension of rent regulation on the grounds of a likely reduction in supply of furnished accommodation. In effect the majority Report in praising the rent regulation machinery and rejecting extension to the furnished sector of security of tenure thereby condoned its very existence as a buffer. The lowest income households were to continue at that time to pay market prices with virtually no protection, security, or financial subsidy in contrast to those protected by rent regulation or receiving financial benefits in other housing tenures.

The incoming Conservative Government in 1970 did not repeal the Rent Act 1968. The Government in the White Paper accompanying the Housing Finance Bill, recognised that 'rent regulation cannot cure a housing shortage. It can only mitigate the effects of the shortage by giving comfort to sitting tenants at the expense of prospective tenants'. The Government saw no inconsistency in their statement:

> So long as there is a shortage of dwellings to let, tenants will need to be protected by rent restriction and given security of tenure.

Under the Housing Finance Act 1972 the provisions

and machinery of 'fair' rent regulation were extended to housing owned by local authorities. Shortly afterwards, the Government introduced rent allowances on a formula related to family income for all tenants in the private unfurnished sector on a similar basis to rent rebates for tenants of local authorities. The initial omission of privately rented households from the public sector rebate scheme was an extraordinary anomaly and subsequently led to successful pressure for allowances to be extended to this sector, which continued to embrace a high and growing proportion of low-income families with little chance of obtaining better housing. The Government had three objections to such an extension. First, that the case-load for rent tribunals would increase unreasonably; second, that it would prove too complex to divorce rent from furniture, fittings and services in calculating allowances; and third, that it would be difficult to give allowances without increasing security of tenure.

In the end the Government introduced a White Paper in December 1972, The Furnished Lettings (Rent Allowances) Bill, which was to provide a special rent allowances procedure for tenants in furnished accommodation. The new Labour Government in 1974 lost no time in embracing the furnished sector within the Rent Acts even though this had been more or less pre-judged as a result of increased security of tenure for this group together with the rent allowances procedure. Nevertheless, it has to be said that criticism of the Rent Act 1974 could only be justified on the grounds that it was another element in the failure of successive governments' policies towards housing and the privately rented sector in particular. To suggest it was wrong on grounds of equity to provide similar rights to security and rent regulation, however ill-conceived in their implications, is to condemn a group of households to discriminatory treatment. Nevertheless, the previous anomalous distinction between furnished and unfurnished tenancies has now been replaced by a new anomaly with a distinction between the resident landlord and non-resident landlord. Under the former category, protection to a tenant is now not given on the basis of furniture provision, but whether the tenancy is deemed, under the three determining conditions, to be part of a landlord's residence or not, so long as the conditions of the residency are satisfied. The converse, however, can never happen, such as a protected tenant losing his protection should the existing new landlord move into residence. The other exceptions to the definition of 'protected tenancy' under the 1974 Act related to student lettings (provided they are let by approved educational institutions) and holiday lettings. Under both categories, the qualifications for exclusion from the legal conditions of the Act are not stringent.

The exemption from the Rent Acts of tenants of resident landlords raised doubts at the time as to the real justification for the Rent Act 1974 in view of the evidence on families in furnished accommodation.

The Francis Committee found that in London, only 17 per cent of households in private furnished rented accommodation were families with children (compared with half of all households). Moreover, the Family Expenditure Survey 1973 shows that in the period immediately prior to the Rent Act, the heads of furnished tenancies in the United Kingdom were relatively well-educated and skilled (56 per cent had a qualification compared with 33 per cent overall). They were also young, with 54 per cent under 30 (compared with 11 per cent overall) and embraced higher socio-economic groups (41 per cent manual, compared with 58 per cent overall). They were also better-off than many local authority tenants and tenants in unfurnished accommodation but less well-off than owner-occupiers. In London over 50 per cent of furnished tenancies were for single people and over one-quarter for two people. The problem, however, relates to regional inequalities, e.g. in London 22 per cent of furnished tenants were in socio-economic group D/E while in some stress areas the figure was as high as 65 per cent.

The Francis Committee found that two main groups of households occupied furnished accommodation:

(a) Households, single people without children, mobile

young and the independent. Relatively high income earners.

(b) Households with children, the poor, who cannot find unfurnished accommodation or a local authority house.

The cheapest accommodation available to this second group was furnished rooms in a run-down area where occupancy rates and sharing were higher. There was a strong presumption that many of these families would not be protected by the Rent Act 1974 as tenants of resident landlords.

Henney's (1975) study of homelessness in Haringey showed clearly that the process of becoming homeless involved losing hold of an insecure tenancy, then sharing with friends and relatives leading to subsequent conflict and ejection from the house. According to Henney, only 15 per cent of the homeless had had a secure tenancy prior to homelessness while 40 per cent had had no tenancy at all. Henney came to the view that it was the generally young, educated and mobile, better-off existing tenants who would benefit most while the very poor in resident accommodation would benefit least. He argued that little reduction in homelessness could be expected for two reasons. First, the homeless are not tenants of non-resident landlords, and second, homelessness was frequently not so much the loss of a home but the difficulty of obtaining another one.

By the latter half of the 1970s, the then Labour Government had become concerned at the effects of the Rent Acts of 1965 and 1974. In the Review of the Rent Acts (1977), the Government concluded:

There is a good deal of criticism that the Rent Acts inhibit the existing stock of houses from being used to full advantage or maintained in a proper condition. It is contended that the effects of the Acts in practice are sometimes unfair to tenants or landlords, or exclude prospective ten-

79

ants and discouarge landlords from keeping properties available for letting. There can be no doubt that the complexity and obscurity of the Acts are a source of frustration and anxiety to landlords, tenants and those responsible for administering and interpreting the legislation.

(Review of the Rent Acts, 1977)

In the Review a number of objectives that the Government believed should be met in any new proposals to halt the decline in the number and quality of rented houses were specified:

(a) to safeguard the interests of existing private tenants;

(b) to ensure that fit private rented houses are properly maintained and kept in repair;

(c) to promote the efficient use of housing and to encourage, for example, the letting of property which might be available for only short lets;

(d) to ensure that the methods and criteria for the determination of rents are tailored to meet the difficulties faced by landlord and tenant;

(e) to simplify the law on private renting and to make for a speedier and more effective resolution of landlord/tenant disputes;

(f) to provide for a legislative framework which maintains a fair balance between the interests of tenants and landlord so that private rented accommodation can contribute effectively to meeting housing needs and choices whilst evolving into social forms involving, and acceptable to, existing landlords and their tenants.

Quite how such diverse and mutually exclusive policy

objectives could be achieved in any reform of legislation was never articulated, yet alone implemented. Two years later, in 1979, the Labour Government was succeeded by a Conservative Government. In view of the Conservative's past objections and hostility to rent control and a manifesto which had expressed a strong predilection for market forces, any expectation that rent control would survive into the 1980s seemed improbable.

CHAPTER EIGHT

FAILURE OF CONSERVATIVES TO DECONTROL

Mr Patten re-affirmed his commitment to maintain the rent acts and emphasised the importance of political consensus if any changes in them were proposed.

Financial Times, 9.12.1986

In Chapters, 3, 4, 5 and 6 we explored in some detail the harmful effects on the supply and demand of private rented housing arising from rent control. The results confirm the theoretical predictions of rent control posed in Chapter 2, and their impact can be seen in the history of rent control in the UK traced through in Chapter 7. Our purpose in this chapter is to examine other influences on the decline of the market for a subsequent analysis of its present plight and characteristics. It is our contention that the Rent Acts and other housing policies have together been largely responsible for the demise of the private rental sector.

Housing Policies Affecting the Private Rented Sector

While the various rents acts acted as a positive disincentive to private provision of rented accommodation other actions of the legislators were tending to pull people away from private renting into council housing and owner-occupancy. Only one action - a limited scheme of rent subsidisation - has acted to offset the bias against private renting. We now review these other policies as a further background to our discussion of policy options in the next two chapters.

Council Housing

As the private rented sector has been gradually killed, the task of providing rental accommodation has been taken over by local authorities for providing housing to lower-income people at below-market rents. Prior to the commencement of sales of council housing, this sector accounted for almost one third of the total housing stock and is still well over one-quarter. The size of this sector in Britain is much larger than in nearly all other countries where policies have been much more conducive to private rental. Total public sector housing spending on local authority housing was approximately £2,500 million in 1985-86.

In addition, Council tenants are also substantial beneficiaries from Housing Benefit which has risen from £400 million in 1981-82 to over £3,200 million in 1985-86, at which level it is projected to remain for the remainder of the decade. The council tenants are not only subsidised by virtue of the nominal rent levied on the property in which they live, but are also beneficiaries according to the relationship between their personal income and this nominal rent. Such enormous state subsidies were neither intended nor anticipated in the past.

Despite a 130 per cent average increase in local authority rents from 1979 to 1984 (after years of virtually no increase at all notwithstanding rapid inflation), public sector tenants still spend a smaller proportion of their income on housing than any other group. In 1983, average unrebated rents paid to local authorities were five per cent lower than housing association tenancies, and thirty-nine per cent lower than regulated furnished tenancies. Average unrebated rents are shown in Table 8.1. Local authority rents now account for 10 per cent of an average manual worker's salary, compared with 7 per cent in 1979.

For the last ten years, local housing authorities have been allowed to fix their own rents. Many Labour-controlled councils raise cash from ratepayers to keep rises to a minimum. The consequence has been a wide disparity in rents. For example, in 1985, two outer London boroughs were charging £13 and £24.50 per week respectively for a similar three-bedroomed house. In England and Wales as a whole, the unrebated rent for a three-bedroomed council house ranged from £22 to £10 a week in 1985.

Rents are therefore not only very low but vary greatly between authorities. Just as we have observed earlier the discrimination that exists in the private rented sector where rents are controlled, so it is clear that in the public sector rent levels depend less on the type and quality of house than on the political colours of the housing authority. But, of course, any increase in rents, either in the public or private sectors, may mean the Exchequer paying yet more than the present £3,200 million plus. Some 65 per cent of all council tenants receive Housing Benefit. Half those are on Supplementary Benefit and so have their rent paid in full.

Table 8.1 Average (unrebated) Rents in 1984

Local Authorities		Private			
		Unfurnished		Furnished	
England and Wales	Greater London	England and Wales	Greater London	England and Wales	Greater London
£	£	£	£	£	£
14.71	16.87	16.62	21.52	24.17	30.38

Mortgage Interest Tax Deductibility
Where there is a comprehensive income tax system in operation it is proper to tax the imputed income from owner-occupied housing and allow mortgage interest payments as a deduction from taxable income. This used to be the case until 1963 even though, for many years prior to that, the Inland Revenue had been collecting revenue

on a base that was much less than the actual imputed income. In 1963 the then Conservative Government made a serious mistake - it removed entirely the need to include imputed income on taxable income without also abolishing mortgage interest deductibility. Income tax relief on qualifying interest on loans for the purchase or improvement of owner-occupied property amounted to approximately £4,750 million in 1985-86.

Exemption from Capital Gains Taxation
While the landlord is subject to taxation on his paltry income from his rental properties and to capital gains taxation if he is fortunate enough to make one when he sells his property, the owner-occupier is (as we just saw) exempt from imputed income taxation and from capital gains taxation. The tax structure strongly favours owner-occupiers and disfavours landlords in all major respects, a bias which is totally unjustified on either equity or efficiency grounds.

The Demise of Privately Rented Housing
While the precise impact of these policies on the decline of the rented sector cannot be measured, there is little doubt that the influences are most certainly adverse. Together with the effects of rent control, they individ-ually and collectively conspire against any reversal in the decline in privately rented housing.

(i)   Size of the market
In Table 8.2 dramatic changes in the tenure and distribu-tion of dwellings since 1914 are shown. While the private rented housing sector has experienced a massive relative decline in its share of total housing from 52 per cent in 1950 to less than 10 per cent in 1986, the shares of owner-occupation and public sector housing have risen from 30 per cent to 63 per cent and 18 per cent to 28 per cent respectively during the same period.

In 1914, about 90 per cent of the total stock of 7.5 million dwellings were let by private owners. During the inter-war period, the proportion of rented housing fell at an increasing rate to about 60 per cent in 1939. This relative decline was mainly due to the rapid increase in owner-occupied and local authority housing, for the absolute net decrease in privately rented housing was only of the order of 0.5 million. While 1.5 million houses were sold for owner-occupation, nearly 1.0 million new or converted houses were added to the private rented sector during that period. Since that time, both the proportion and absolute size of the stock have fallen dramatically, so that by 1986 the proportion was less than 10 per cent, accounting for less dwellings and households than ever before. Sales for owner-occupation have been important but in contrast to the inter-war period, there have been only 0.4 million new or converted houses added to the private rented sector in the whole of the post-war period.

Table 8.2 Distribution of Dwellings by Tenure (Percentages) (UK)

	Owner-occupied	Rented from public authorities or New Town Corporations	Rented from private owners
	%	%	%
1914	10	-	90
1950	29	18	53
1960	42	26	32
1975	53	31	16
1985	63	28	9

Source: Housing and Construction Statistics 1985

Failure of Conservatives to Decontrol

In fact, the increase in the share of owner-occupation and public authority housing have been more dramatic than appears in Table 8.2. It has not only been the share of the privately rented sector which has fallen as a result of new building for other tenures, but the actual stock of housing in this sector has been acquired by other tenures over the years. For example, the total net gain in housing units for owner-occupation alone has actually exceeded the total number of all new housing units in some years. In other words, it has not just been the almost complete absence of new building for private renting which has prompted its decline, but substantial net losses of such accommodation to other tenures, especially owner-occupation.

By contrast, there has been practically no investment in private rented housing. The years of rent control and security of tenure have destroyed the sector and discouraged any new investment or initiatives. Britain must be unique among the western industrialised countries in financing homes for rent almost exclusively through the public sector.

(ii) Landlords and Tenants

Only very limited aggregate data exist on the types, age and incomes of landlords and tenants. According to the successive Censuses there is a wide diversity of households in rented housing and a marked contrast in types of tenant in furnished (resident and non-resident landlords) and unfurnished (regulated and controlled) tenancies, as defined under the 1965 Rent Act and discussed in Chapter 7. Tenants in the unfurnished sector were typically elderly, on low incomes, and had occupied their homes over many years. By contrast, the furnished sector comprised tenants who were typically young, single, mobile and with above average incomes for their age groups. A sample survey by Paley (1976) of selected local areas of England and Wales containing more privately rented households than owner-occupied households, revealed that landlords fell into several distinct groups: resident landlords 12 per cent, non-resident landlords 35 per cent, companies 25 per cent, charities and housing associations 15 per cent, non-charitable trusts and executors 6 per cent and public bodies 7 per cent. Compared with individual landlords, corporate and other organisational landlords each tended to own a number of premises. Different types of landlord had different motivations for letting and Paley detected three broad groups: (a) lettings made by resident landlords were regarded as part of the landlord's own home and they were not in general looking to the rent received as an economic return on the value of property occupied; (b) lettings made by housing associations (eligible for public subsidy), public bodies and charities were regarded as provision for those in need or for employees and again, no economic return on property occupied was sought; and (c) lettings made by non-resident individuals and companies (in total over 60 per cent of landlords) were in general viewed in terms of an economic investment. These land-lords commonly felt that an adequate rent should cover a return on the value of the property and very few consid-ered the 'fair' rent received as adequate.

(iii) Age and Condition of Dwellings
According to the 1981 England and Wales House Condition Survey, 60 per cent of privately rented dwellings were built before 1919 compared with less than 35 per cent of the owner-occupied and less than 4 per cent of the local authority housing stock. The majority of the remaining 40 per cent of privately rented houses were built in the inter-war period. Some 30 per cent of privately rented houses lacked one or more basic amenities, 30 per cent were in disrepair, and 20 per cent were statutorily unfit for habitation.

(iv) Geographical Distribution
The geographical distribution of the privately rented sector is uneven and tends to be concentrated within the larger inner city areas. London alone accounts for over 25 per cent of privately rented dwellings and about 37 per cent of all households in furnished dwellings. A number of the larger University cities contain a relatively high

proportion of privately let dwellings.

A Way Forward?

In the face of such adverse market characteristics, what hope exists for a reversal of the worsening trends in rented housing? For long embattled by the effects of the Rent Acts, it is now expedient to explore what options may exist.

Following the Review of the Rent Acts 1977 no new legislation emerged until the return of a Conservative Government in 1979. In the Housing Act 1980, the short-hold tenancy was introduced. Under such a tenancy a landlord is able to gain repossession of rented property after a specified time. The minimum period is one year. Originally, it had been a requirement that a fair rent should be applied to shorthold tenancies but this was later waived, except in London. While tenants can appeal to a rent officer it is no longer necessary to register a fair rent at the commencement of a shorthold tenancy.

While these new shorthold tenancies have overcome two major impediments to landlord letting, viz, full security of tenure and potential capital loss, they have not been sufficient to induce landlords to return to the housing market. Certainly, for a landlord, the fact that he no longer faces risks of considerable capital loss is a major attraction. In non-shorthold tenancies, a tenant can apply successfully to a Rent Officer for a fair rent to be set and full security of tenure.

Todd's (1986) survey of parish lettings between 1982 and 1984 yields a number of interesting results:

(a) Among respondents to the survey, only 4 per cent of tenants against 14 per cent of landlords of recent lettings considered their tenancies to be shorthold.

(b) Conversely, 21 per cent of tenants against 8 per cent of landlords, believed themselves to enjoy full tenure within the stated fixed term.

In addition to the shorthold tenancy, the Housing Act

1980 introduced a new 'assured tenancy' which was to allow landlords 'approved' by the Government to let at freely negotiated rents. Lettings were to be subject to the Landlord and Tenant Act, 1954, but not to the Rent Acts. This scheme has now been in operation for some years and some two hundred landlords have now, in fact, been approved - builders, insurance companies, building societies and housing associations - but they have had little impact on the rented sector as a whole.

While both the shorthold and assured tenancies have provided some move towards deregulation, their use has clearly not been widespread. Certainly they have done little, so far, to reverse the trend in the decline of the rented sector. In London, licences have been used proportionately more than elsewhere, while the use of shorthold tenancies appears to be proportionately greater outside London.

In short, the Housing Act, 1980 and its new forms of tenure have had some effect in cushioning the worsening situation but their impact should not be overstated. For example, as will be examined later, the Rent Acts encouraged the letting of accommodation to the young and mobile. The fact that the Housing Act 1980 has encouraged a further boost to this trend owes less to the intrinsic virtues of the Act than to the release of a valve from the pressure arising from pernicious and counterproductive Rent Acts.

More recently, under the 1986 Housing Act, the Government has lifted two restrictions on private landlords as part of the Government's 'right-to-rent' campaign. Landlords are now able to impose higher rents agreed by a rent officer immediately, instead of having to phase them in over two years. Also, landlords in Greater London will be able to let property on a yearly basis without needing to register a fair rent with a rent officer. Interestingly, and relevant to our proposals contained in Chapter 10, tenants eligible for rent rebates will be unaffected.

A further aspect of the Housing Act 1986 has been the extension of the approved landlord scheme. This

Failure of Conservatives to Decontrol

potentially can mean the refurbishment of empty dwellings to approved standards by approved landlords, and let on assured tenancies, offering security of tenure, subject to five year rent reviews, just like most commercial leases. Such a move raises the question of whether the Government might soon abolish the right of secure tenants to hand on tenancies to their children. Clearly, such an initiative would imply that the pace of renewal of the rented sector would be set by the life expectancy of existing tenants and the supply of approvable landlords. However, while we would be churlish to criticise these modest reforms as a step towards more radical reforms, it has to be said that the 1986 Housing Act has not gone far enough to arrest all the criticisms we have identified in rent control, let alone reverse the appalling impact of control on labour mobility.

Too often, there are those sympathetic to reform but who argue caution. Two major arguments are advanced. First, it is said that radical reform, e.g. complete abolition, is politically impossible. The reasoning is rarely articulated. In Chapter 10, we point out that those who propagate such a view should remember that protected tenants enjoy their rights at the expense of the homeless and the job-seekers. Second, more radical reforms than those contained in the Housing Act 1986 are cautioned on the grounds that a change of government would wipe out any 'benefits' of reform attaching to landlords. Such a possibility leads gradualists to propose that reforms should embrace 'cross-party' support. Such a justification has not prevented the Conservative Government from privatising an increasing number of enterprises. This has not only been popular among the electorate but the Government has gained even greater support for such measures in the face of Labour proposals to re-nationalise at original share issue prices. In short, a policy of piecemeal reforms justified on the basis of 'cross party' support to reduce the alleged risks of dramatic reversals of policy and impact on landlords is shilly-shallying at its worst. The Rent Acts of 1965 and 1974 were imposed by Labour Governments within a year of their respective elections! Did they seek 'cross party' support?

In the light of the prevailing legislation it is now time to examine in Chapters 9 and 10 alternative proposals for reform.

CHAPTER NINE

POLICY OPTIONS FOR REFORM

... this decline is the entirely predictable result of rent control and rent regulation, since 'fair' (or controlled) rents do not give an adequate return on capital except to a few landlords who can obtain implicit non-monetary returns. The sector's traditional role of fostering labour migration and facilitating housing mobility has therefore been all but destroyed.

Patrick Minford, Michael Peel and Paul Ashton

Faced with a situation of persistent decline of the privately rented sector, what can the state do? A number of possibilities present themselves, but they all pose difficulties.

Policy proposals to at least protect the remaining rented property have centred on either the complete social ownership of housing through government take-over and responsibility for this housing stock and tenants (Wicks, 1973), or proposals for a revitalisation of the private rented sector.

Either municipalisation or reform of rent regulation would undoubtedly require similar supporting measures if a semblance of order and permanence is ever to be achieved - improvement grants beyond those existing, incentives to new construction, and even tenants' participation. But the real issue is whether the government is to assume direct responsibility for this housing group or whether the private sector is to be

Policy Options for Reform

provided with the climate conducive to a healthy rented sector unfettered by the current severe restraints in government regulations.

A. Municipalisation

This policy objective would necessitate gradual and complete municipalisation of all privately rented property financed by long-term loan issues together with fairly considerable Exchequer subsidies to bring the acquired properties up to local authority housing standards. While the last Labour Government ruled out municipalisation, proponents would argue that this is the only solution for the privately rented sector, mainly on the grounds of their objection to the private landlord, per se. Their belief that the 'housing problem' will only be solved when all rented property is under government ownership accords to demands for the rationalisation of rents. Housing would be allocated by need, and not price, to provide for the reduction of under-occupation, and the implementation of policies towards reducing stress through repairs and modernisation. If the local authorities were to take over the remaining burden the costs would be considerable and they have always been understandably unenthusiastic. They would assume immediate and uncompromising responsibility for the dwellings which, under government minimum standards, are inadequate, requiring massive renovation, if not clearance, and a new home for tenants. Even if central government finance was forthcoming, the local authorities would be required to undertake the responsibility for implementation of policy through acquisition and landlord 'compensation', rehousing tenants during renovation and repairs, clearing condemned houses and the rehousing of families against an existing background of homelessness and record local authority housing waiting lists.

The arguments for a municipal take-over of the existing stock have been summarised by Murie (1976) who has contended that such a policy could provide:

(a) increased control over the sector and occupancy

standards since muncipalisation would automatically ensure that the fair rent system and tenancy rights were automatically extended to all existing tenants;

(b) improved allocation systems through allocation according to local authority perceived 'need' rather than by a subtle combination, according to Murie, of 'rents, search and queueing costs which tended to favour young persons with higher levels of incomes and experience in particular local housing markets'.

Proponents of municipalisation have neither costed their proposals, and perhaps more relevant, nor have they questioned in any depth the reasons for bizarre allocation systems under a controlled rental system. In any case with so many local authority houses in poor condition it is doubtful whether the supply of improved properties would rise in inner city areas.

It is not surprising that the notion of municipalisation, once so popular on the 'left', is now intellectually dead as a realistic answer to the decline of the private rented sector.

B. Expansion of the Voluntary Service
Less dramatic, but similar in effect, have been proposals for an expansion of Housing Associations in order to replace private lets. Implementation of such proposals imply considerable public finance through one or a combination of the following: higher rents, Exchequer subsidies, or 'voluntary' finance from institutional bodies. Whether the associations have the ability to cater for additional housing units is questionable, particularly in respect of young transient groups.

In the Housing Act 1980, some attempt was made to encourage the provision of rented housing by financial institutions through the introduction of the assured tenancy scheme. Under the scheme, landlords approved by the Government are permitted to build new housing to let at rents and on terms freely negotiated in the market, but subject to the Landlord and Tenant Act 1954. The hope of

97

this scheme also lay in encouragement to housing associations to apply for registration as approved bodies. The scheme has had little success so far although the largest recent participant was an association, Abbey Housing Association, with some 70 lettings out of a total of about 700 in 1986. The Government expects the number to grow to 1500 by 1988. However, progress is remarkably slow and the scheme has had virtually no impact on the rented sector, even though the scheme is outside normal rent regulation.

C. Reform within the Present Legal Framework of Control

In an analysis by Cooper and Stafford (1980), a number of possibilities were examined using a model introduced in Chapter 7 and represented by Figure 9.1.

(i) Control Rents at P_1

Rent control at P_1 would represent a perpetuation of the present policy of 'fair rents' and theoretically implies the transference of P_1BAP_2 suppliers' surplus to consumers and prevents them 'exploiting' the short-run shortage. While the rent is 'fair' in that it fully meets the long-run supply price of OS_1 units, it in no way provides an incentive to suppliers to increase supply, even in the long run. Moreover, it is potentially unstable, for landlords are well aware that there are OS_1 people willing to pay a rent of P_2 or more and will accordingly attempt to circumvent rent legislation. Moreover, once the rent is controlled at P_1, it will be politically difficult to remove the control for there will be an excess demand of S_1T (OT families are willing and able to pay the 'fair rent') and a queue will emerge.

In the case of those landlords who attempt to evade the law, some of the enhanced consumers' surplus will find its way back to them. A black market will emerge with such practices as key-money and payment for fixtures and fittings. Some families are even willing to pay in excess of a rent of P_2. Landlords will also attempt to increase their utility from rationing by prejudice (colour, creed, a

Policy Options for Reform

ban on children and pets, etc.) in order to reduce the potential risks of being suddenly subject to rent regulation. Nevertheless, without Government provision of housing, S_1T families will still go homeless or be forced to share housing in extended family groups.

(ii) Control Rents at P_3
A fair rent set at P_3 would represent market equilibrium in the absence of the 'temporary' supply constraint. Moreover, it has the advantage that it offers landlords some inducement to expand supplies in the long run under increasing cost conditions and consumers are not being asked to pay more than the 'normal' long-run cost. On the other hand, a shortage of S_1Z units would still remain with S_1T homeless in the short run and ZT in the long run.

(iii) Permit Rents to Rise to P_2
This would mean effective abandonment of 'fair rents' in the short run, given the expectation that in the long run equilibrium would be achieved at P_3. In the short run, landlords would gain considerable surplus but, given the freedom of entry, there would apparently be a strong incentive to supply OZ units. No rationing other than the ability and willingness to pay is necessary or probable but, even in the long run, there would remain unmet need of ZT.

(iv) Subsidise Demand
Under this strategy the state could abolish rent controls but accept that 'needs' outstrip ability to pay and so subsidise demand either at a flat rate per unit of housing or an ad valorem subsidy. In Figure 7.1, the removal of control at P_1 and the subsidising of demand by P_2P_4 per unit would, in the short run, increase rents to P_4. In the long run the shift of the demand curve to the right would yield a new equilibrium level which coincided with need of OT units at the rent of P_5. Both DD and D_1D_1 demand curves will 'kink' at OT units for the same reasons given under Figure 9.1, except that in the case of D_1D_1 it is assumed that every family with assistance can pay a rent

99

Policy Options for Reform

of P_5. Demand, therefore, is perfectly inelastic up to and including the 'fair rent' level of P_5.

The state would pay the difference between the tenant's payment of rent P_1 and the landlord's receipt of P_5. The relative gains to the tenant and the landlord will depend upon the elasticities of supply and demand. In Figure 9.1, the tenant is now paying P_1P_3 less than he would have in the former equilibrium position and the landlord is receiving P_3P_5 more. The greater the elasticity of supply and the lower the elasticity of demand, the greater will be the relative gain to the tenant from any given subsidy and vice-versa.

Figure 9.1

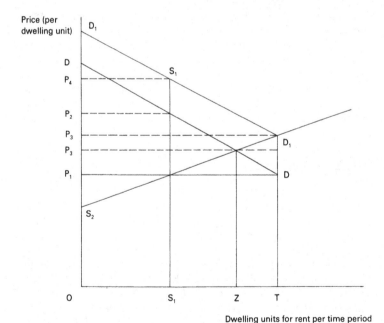

Dwelling units for rent per time period

(v) Extension of Exemptions from Powers of the
     Rent Acts
Under the 1974 Rent Act, it is possible for landlords to let
furnished rental housing through recognised local or national organisations (e.g. education, armed forces) and be
exempted from the powers of the act. There is scope for
extension but it is more likely to add to discrimination
than reduce it. This is because the market would be
segmented between those tenants in education or the
armed forces (young and mobile) and thereby enhance
their housing possibilities but militate against other
groups of tenants.

D.   Major Modifications of the 'Fair Rent' System
Maclennan (1980) has indicated some measures which he
believes could improve the operation of the private rental
market within the present United Kingdom regulated
system. Under a new regime of an informed staff, explicit
procedures and operational rules, he suggests, rent
controls need not mean the end of the private rental
sector:

1. All private lets should be covered by regis-
    tration and the Rent Acts.

2. Landlords, or companies, should be issued
    with a licence to let which would not be
    transferable. The licence would be with-
    drawn if landlords were found to violate
    the service provision, rent or improvement
    clauses of their individual lets or be found
    guilty of harassment or illegal practices.

3. When properties were registered or licen-
    sed the Rent Assessment Committee would
    discuss with the landlord the level of ser-
    vices to be provided and improvements to
    be enacted and these would be allowed for
    in assessing rents.

4. Rents for individual properties would be assessed by a professional staff of valuers and cost accountants who would be employed by the rent service and whose salaries and costs would be paid for by a licence fee. The introduction of a detailed consideration of costs would allow marginal rents to rise, but the system may not wish to penalise infra-marginal landlords.

5. Rents would be related to capital values with no scarcity factors to distort inter-sectoral tenure choices or to prevent long-run adjustment.

6. A fair real rate of return on capital would be allowed, possibly indexed to allowed returns on nationalised industries, and with rents linked to a chosen general price index. Or alternatively, they could be linked to returns on equities since housing asset values are likely to appreciate.

7. Security of tenure provisions would be related to the type of licence held by landlords. Long-term letting landlords would be allowed a small premium (say 1%) on rents and rates of return. There could be limits to the number of occasions on which short-term licences could be renewed for a particular landlord and tenants.

8. Capital appreciation on housing assets would be excluded from the assessment of letting returns, as such rises, in part, also reflect the rising replacement cost of landlords' capital. Disinvesting landlords would, of course, be subject to capital gains tax as

at the present time.

9.   A rental sector inspection service should
        be introduced to investigate properties to
        ensure that the terms of licences are being
        observed. This service could also investi-
        gate tenants' and landlords' grievances.

As an option, Maclennan believes that if the above:

>   proposals were adopted a rationally plan-
>   ned private sector of furnished rental could
>   be sustained and indeed expanded. A
>   professionally orientated and informed set
>   of assessment councils, supplemented by an
>   effective policing system, could then pro-
>   ceed to operate the rental sector with
>   fairness and precision.

All the above proposals ranging from municipalisation
to extension and/or modification of the present Acts, fail
to overcome the allocation damages of the existing system of rent controls. The 1980 Housing Act which introduced shorthold tenancies has had virtually no effect on
the decline in this sector. Theoretical analysis, elaborated
earlier, makes quite clear that under the present control
of rents no increase in the supply of rental housing can be
forthcoming.

E.   Abandonment of Rent Regulation
The present system of rent control is justified on the most
slender grounds and should not continue in its present
form. A radical and positive policy needs to be devised
and implemented that will lead to a free market in
private rented housing. Repeal of the Rent Acts and less
government intervention in the rented sector is necessary
if long-term revisions are to be implemented and the free
market is allowed to re-emerge after an absence of
seventy years.
        The risks associated with present legislation have

Policy Options for Reform

evidently induced landlords to cease letting at the earliest opportunity, whilst those who continue to let may attempt to minimise the risk of financial loss by letting to the more transient groups of tenants - students, holiday-makers, etc. - and by reducing the standard of mainten-ance of their property. Either one of these effects is sufficient to militate against successive governments' main objectives for the rented housing market, but in the face of such adversity it is perhaps amazing that the sector survives at all.

CHAPTER TEN

PATH TO ABOLITION

... in rental housing abolish all rent controls, instantly.

The Economist, 3.1.1987

We are quite unequivocal about what must happen. Britain stands out from most countries in the world in that it retains a system of rigid rental market controls that have asphyxiated the private rental housing sector. While other countries removed their wartime controls, Britain did not. Moves in the direction in the late 1950s were reversed in the mid-1960s. This continuation of controls, combined with other factors, has caused a dramatic decline in this important sector of the housing market. Without doubt, rental market controls must be abolished. The only questions that remain are these:

- Should controls on rents and evictions be removed gradually or, as we prefer, in one fell swoop?

- What, if any, amount and form of compensation, and paid by and to whom, should be made? (We resist the temptation to suggest that landlords should be compensated rather than tenants.)

- Should decontrol occur alone or as part of a major change in policy involving the abolition of virtually all the subsidies and controls affecting the housing market?

105

Path to Abolition

- After decontrol, is there a role for government in the private rental housing market?

In this final chapter, we attempt to answer these important questions.

Approaches to Housing Policy

The 'ideal' way to approach housing policy is to take an overall view. The policy-maker should ask what is the objective of government intervention in the housing market and then formulate an overall policy stance which achieves the objective(s) at the minimum possible economic cost. In doing so, the existing set of policies should be largely ignored. These only become important when it gets to the stage of determining how to implement the chosen policy. Implementation of the new policy will necessitate scrapping the existing set of policies if, as in the case of Britain, they are ill-advised and contradictory. This will involve the creation of a complex pattern of gains and losses to individuals. After the new policy is in place some will be compensated for their losses while others will not.

This is not the way that things usually get done. In virtually all countries there is a confusing array of housing policies which have been developed over time, largely as a consequence of pragmatic and disjointed decisions made by governments under the influence of various lobby groups, including of course, civil servants. Even when housing policy is looked at as a whole, the constraints placed on the reviewers usually rule-out an efficient and equitable outcome. The review process almost inevitably becomes heavily politicised, either at the review stage or after the recommendations reach government (or both) and any results are of a patchwork kind that do not get to the heart of the problems.

When we look at housing policy in Britain it is difficult to find one aspect that is not the result of political pragmatism. The history of rental market control and decontrol is a classic case where economic principle has been totally lacking from the decision-making process. Having killed private renting, governments were forced to build up public renting to such an extent that it has become more than three times as large as the private rented sector. The development of council housing has been marked by indiscriminate targeting of benefits and insufficient attention to the social consequences of large geographical concentrations of low-income people in inappropriate housing.

A. Removing Rent and Eviction Control Only
Most discussions of decontrolling the private rental market for housing tend to concentrate on this single act while paying insufficient attention to the other policies impinging on housing and individual well-being. Various schemes have been devised over the years that are designed to lighten the load on tenants by either replacing subsidies from landlords with those from the state or by graduating decontrol over a period of time. Our own approach attempts to separate the issue of income maintenance from that of housing policy.

The most recent proposal for decontrol is that suggested by Martin Ricketts (1986). This involves giving sitting tenants clearly-defined property rights to the stream of subsidy from rent control for a period of, say, ten years. Tenants would have the right to remain in their property at a controlled rent for the nominated period or sell the right to whomever they chose (e.g. another tenant, the landlord or a housing association) for a lump sum. All new tenancies would be decontrolled completely. The scheme is designed to enhance mobility, restore the incentive to invest in rental housing, partially protect the tenant's interest and ultimately result in the complete end of rent and eviction controls. All this would be achieved while being politically palatable.

We applaud this scheme as a serious attempt to ease the pain of the transition from a regime of rent control to one of a free market. Similar schemes have been proposed in the past. The late Sir Roy Harrod (1947) suggested that sitting tenants be entitled to the difference between market and controlled rents for a period of ten years whether they stay in the dwelling or not. The landlord would be taxed the rent difference and this amount paid to the tenant for ten years. As in Ricketts' scheme, new tenancies would be decontrolled completely. The only difference is that all amounts are in flows per period rather than capitalised present values. Frank Paish (1952) proposed a variant of Harrod's plan where some of the tax on landlords did not go to sitting tenants but was deployed elsewhere - 25 per cent in an allowance to landlords to maintain their properties and some of the rest to fund an income maintenance programme.

The Paish variant of Harrod's scheme is preferable to that of Ricketts in a number of respects. It has more chance of being embraced warmly by landlords who now get something out of it - the means to maintain better their properties. Secondly, it aids tenants as well because they will have the benefits of better maintained living conditions. The stimulus to better maintenance in fact, benefits everyone. Thirdly, it creates some funds that could be used in helping any real victims of higher free market rents. New tenants, renting at market rates, could be embittered by the generosity of Ricketts' scheme with no provision for them at all.

While these types of schemes are motivated by a desire to end ultimately rent control and to reap some immediate benefits while not losing too many votes for the sponsoring government, the degree of generosity to tenants must be looked at very carefully. In one sense, sitting tenants are not really a worthy group at all, having already enjoyed a subsidy (sometimes of a large magnitude for a long period of time) at the expense of their hapless landlords. This enforced transfer has no clear moral justification, particularly when considered in the light of the circumstances of many of the tenants and landlords concerned. It is often not a 'Robin Hood' type redistribution at all.

Consider the following matrix of wealth of tenants and landlords (Table 10.1). It is only in category B that rent control produces a redistribution with any moral defensibility. In category C, poor landlords subsidise rich tenants, and the other categories, involving poor-to-poor (A) and rich-to-rich (D) subsidies should not be very encouraging to the advocates of rent control. Our knowledge of the attributes of landlords and tenants, discussed in Chapter 8, does not encourage us to think that category B is the normal pattern of redistribution.

Except in a political sense, the number of tenants deserving of compensation from landlords is nil, but the number that society might wish to compensate - at the expense of taxpayers in general - could be quite large. We worry about the approach which places the burden on landlords, even if they ultimately will be freed of the obligation to subsidise tenants.

Table 10.1   The Redistribution from Rent Control

		Landlords	
		Poor	Rich
Tenants	Poor	A	B
	Rich	C	D

If decontrol were to occur 'overnight' or at one fell swoop, with no change to any of the existing subsidy arrangements, many would be automatically compensated by both the current system of housing benefits (many tenants would become eligible when their rents rose) and by other elements of the welfare system. Only those tenants who were, in a sense, able to afford the market rent would be ineligible for compensation. This would be an improvement in that the state would take over the responsibility for subsidies from landlords and subsidies would be far better directed. The aggregate increase in subsidy payments would be less than the transfer from tenants to landlords. Such a transfer of the burden of subsidy from landlords to government is justified. The housing benefit system is supposed to be capable, technically and administratively, of providing support to lower income tenants. Those who argue, however, these costs to be too high for government to bear are merely offering a cynical defence of the status quo. Government has the apparatus and duty to provide help to the lower income households at a level and degree it deems appropriate; it is not the duty or responsibility of the landlord.

In short, we are arguing that if decontrol were to occur within the context of other housing subsidies remaining (and this is not our first-best solution), compensation for the most needy tenants would occur automatically. Other tenants have no moral or other basis to expect to be compensated and should not be considered in this regard, and certainly should not be compensated at the expense of landlords. We feel that Martin Ricketts' scheme is too generous to tenants, indiscriminate in its compensation and involves an unwarranted continuation of the tax on landlords[1].

B.   A General Review of Housing Policy?
There is no doubt in our minds that the demise of the private rental housing market is, in large part, the consequence of government interference not only in this sector directly but also in regard to owner-occupancy and in the provision of council housing. In the case of owner-occupancy and council housing the source of the subsidies is taxpayers at large while in the case of private renting it is the landlord. This fact is of considerable importance in explaining the dramatic decline in private renting in Britain.

Our first-best policy is for the Government to get out of the rented housing market completely; abolishing rent control, reforming mortgage interest tax deductibility and removing council housing subsidies. Any 'welfare' that remains should be directed at those on low incomes and be totally divorced from housing per se. Government interference in the housing market must be branded as an abject failure by any set of criteria and each attempt to 'improve' the situation seems to make things worse.

Even in this century there was a time when the entire housing market in Britain was virtually free of any significant intervention by the government. Gradually - beginning in 1916 - the role of the state became more and more pervasive with intervention in the owner-occupancy sector (heavily subsidised since the early 1960s when imputed income from owner-occupied housing ceased to be subject to income tax but mortgage interest remained deductible for tax purposes) and council housing (which reached nearly one-third of all dwellings in 1980 and has since declined slightly because of council house sales to owner-occupiers). Private rentals are also subsidised directly by government in circumstances where the land-lord cannot be called on more than at present. The tendency has been one of subsidising all sectors rather than none. If tenure-neutrality was the aim it has not been achieved. This is because the rates of subsidy differ markedly within and between tenure types.

One approach might be to go beyond the recently revised housing benefit scheme and to aim for true tenure-neutrality where all segments of the market are subsidised at the same rate and at the expense of the taxpayer in general. This could involve inter alia, the removal of rent control and its replacement by an across-the-board rent subsidy to tenants paid from the Treasury coffers. This subsidy would have to be equated with that for council housing, involving an adjustment of rents in that sector to conform with the general rate of subsidy. This would all have to be combined with a properly targeted income-maintenance scheme available to all those meeting the criteria irrespective of type of housing tenure.

Depending on the general rate of housing subsidy chosen and the generosity of income maintenance, this scheme may or may not result in an increase in public outlays, including tax expenditures. However, when we stop and think about the general subsidy approach to tenure-neutrality we begin to realise how silly it would be to do it this way. Why not achieve tenure-neutrality by setting the across-the-board housing subsidy at precisely zero?

Private rents would almost all rise by amounts ranging from very little in the case of fair rents where housing is not particularly scarce, to a lot in other cases. Virtually all private tenants would pay more, some receiving a double shock where rent subsidies were previously paid. Compensation would occur for those that were eligible for general income maintenance but many would pay more in an outright sense - perhaps much more, landlords would definitely gain and taxpayers in general would lose if income maintenance payments exceeded savings on rent subsidies.

Council house rents would also rise, again by varying amounts but probably more uniformly. Housing benefits would also be removed. Many would receive compensation under income maintenance and the effect on taxpayers would be ambiguous, but probably negative.

Reintroduction of taxation on the net imputed income from owner-occupation (i.e. mortgage interest deductibility would be allowed as a housing cost) could raise the housing costs of many owner-occupiers buying their homes and may have a downward effect on property values. Taxpayers would almost certainly gain in net terms as savings in tax expenditures would probably exceed any income maintenance payments to lower income groups in this sector.

Our guess is that society would gain overall from the removal of all housing subsidies. We have shown in previous chapters the costs in economic efficiency associated with rent control. Similarly efficiency gains would flow from the abolition of other subsidies which distort production and consumption decisions, impede mobility, etc. Thousands of millions of pounds worth of extra output could flow from the enhancement of labour mobility alone (see Minford et al, 1986). The gainers could easily compensate the losers from this set of changes with a social gain left over. Of course, society may not wish to compensate all the losers from the change. The income

112

maintenance scheme would mean that subsidies were directed where they were most needed.

The political repercussions of such a broad change may not be as severe as from individually tinkering with particular parts of the subsidy apparatus. Every small attempt to decontrol the rental housing market or reform the extent of mortgage interest deductibility is met with a howl of protest from those affected (including, we suspect, the bureaucrats who run these schemes). From the viewpoint of the recipients, their degree of acceptance of the loss of their subsidy could be enhanced by the knowledge that others are also losing. Threatening only one group can be seen as being horizontally inequitable.

Intervention after Decontrol

Free markets do not necessarily work as smoothly as in an economics text book. When demand for housing increases in a locality because of population movements, income increases, subsidies or whatever, rents will tend to rise. It is in this circumstance that greedy profiteering landlords become the target of abuse - they receive the blame for rising rents and it is often said that private rental markets are 'imperfect'. Housing is a commodity which is in relatively fixed supply in the short run and this is why rents rise when demand increases. This is not an imperfection - it is a technical fact of life.

Other alleged 'imperfections' are also identified by those advocating intervention - insecurity of tenure, intrusive behaviour by landlords, etc. Many instances of such allegations could be cited, but the Commission of Inquiry into Poverty (1975) in Australia provides a good example. The Commission unambiguously rejected rent control on the grounds that 'We do not agree that rent control is in the long-term interest of tenants' (p.161). This was because:

(i)   landlords will 'have clear incentive to get rid of tenants'

113

Path to Abolition

(ii) It 'can lead to landlords attempting to cut costs by not spending money on maintenance'

(iii) There is an 'overall effect of a sharp reduction in the supply of rental accommodation'

Nonetheless, the Commission did advocate state intervention in the private rental housing market (p.162):

> The cheap private rental market has many other unsatisfactory aspects such as insecurity of tenure, illegal retention of bond money, biased leases, and legislation which gives tenants few legal rights.

What then is the role of the state which does not engage in heavy-handed rent and eviction controls? Our discussion will revolve around the following areas of possible activity - setting of 'fair rents', security of tenure and the enforcement of private contracts.

The only type of rent control that we would even consider is one that adjudicated in the event of dispute between a landlord and a tenant over whether the rent was actually a 'market rent' or not. This could be appealed to by either the tenant or the landlord. The major criteria the 'rent controller' would draw on are the rents on comparable premises, current property values and current cost levels. Even this type of control causes us some worries as it creates machinery that could be applied to more damaging ends. We totally reject any notion of fair rent (like that applied in Britain) that ignores the scarcity value of dwellings. The disallowance of scarcity as a factor in rent-setting robs the community of the signal that leads to the elimination of that 'abnormal' scarcity by the creation of new supply.

Security of tenure is another major concern of tenants. It is interesting to observe that this usually becomes a concern when rents are regulated - only then do landlords have an incentive to evict tenants for reasons other than their unsuitability (e.g. because of damage to house, failure to pay rent, annoyance to neighbours, etc.). That is why rent and eviction controls usually go hand-in-hand - if there is one there must also be the other. We would like to see security of tenure become, as it traditionally was, a matter of private contractual arrangement between landlord and tenant. Landlords would ensure the tenant security of tenure for a specified period of time as long as the tenant observed certain conditions. The only role for the state would be one of providing the machinery for the enforcement of voluntary private contracts.

We do not believe that regulation of the kind that refrains from rigid rent control but does control conditions of evictions, security deposits, etc. is in the interests of either landlords or tenants. The role of the state should end with the establishment of a tribunal to adjudicate between the parties where there is a dispute over the contract, such as when the landlord refuses to return a security deposit.

When the state interferes with the nature of the contract itself this cannot be in the interests of the parties - if the state's contract is superior, then why has it not been adopted by the parties under voluntary agreement between them? In demonstrating this proposition we apply some simple analysis originally due to Ross Parish (1980). Consider Figure 10.1 which shows the demand curve and the supply curve for rental accommodation before the intervention of the state ($D_0 D_0$ and $S_0 S_0$). The initial rent is P_0 and quantity Q_0. Now suppose that the authorities impose a contract on the parties which involves giving tenants various rights, but does not control rents. Tenants value these rights positively so that their willingness-to-pay for rental accommodation rises, the demand curve shifting to $D_1 D_1$. However, these rights impose a cost on landlords in that they have less control over the use of their property and must meet certain obligations. The supply curve shifts up by the amount of these costs (per unit) to $S_1 S_1$.

As we have drawn it, the upward shift in the supply curve is greater than that in the demand curve so that

Path to Abolition

rent has risen by more than the increased willingness-to-pay. Quantity traded also falls, from Q_0 to Q_1, unless prevented by the security of tenure provisions. Not only are tenants worse off (P_1-P_0 > value of rights) but landlords are also disadvantaged. The rise in rental is less than the extra per unit costs borne by them. This unhappy result must emerge unless there are significant informational problems in the market. The imposed contract must be inferior or else it would not have to be imposed - the iron fist is less effective than the invisible hand.

Figure 10.1

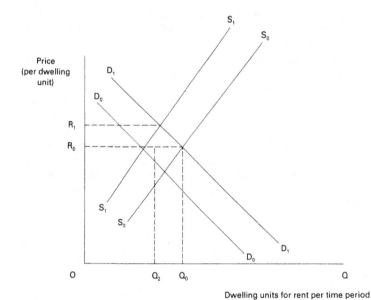

Dwelling units for rent per time period

Perhaps the state has a role in advising tenants and landlords about the pitfalls that might be encountered in formulating contracts. This could be accomplished by establishing a tenants' and landlords' advisory service attached to its tribunal. The tribunal may also have a role in setting what are effectively market rents when the parties cannot agree. However, even this proposal is of a tentative kind as we have severe doubts about state intervention.

In conclusion, we see that the state does have a role in providing legal redress where contracts made between parties have not been upheld and also to protect landlords and tenants alike from the unscrupulous. We submit however that the state has no need to perpetuate and enforce a statutory rent-setting machinery. It is to this end that we urge an early repeal of all rent control and regulation and the introduction of comprehensive voluntary rental market contracts.

Note

1. Of course, not all landlords actually bear the tax. Some landlords will have purchased properties with a sitting tenant and will have paid a price reflecting its value under rental market control. They would be making a normal return from their investment and would receive a windfall from decontrol.

BIBLIOGRAPHY

Albon, R.P. (1981) An economic evaluation of rent control and other rental housing market policies in Australia, Doctoral thesis, Department of Economics, Australian National University

Bank of New South Wales (1953) 'Implications of rent control', Bank of New South Wales, 12, February, 10-13. Reprinted in R.P. Albon (ed.) Rent control: cost and consequences, Centre for Independent Studies, Sydney, Ch. 7 (ii), 1980

Begg, D., Fischer, S. and Dornbusch, R. (1984) Economics, British edn, McGraw-Hill, London

Browning, E.K. and Browning, J.M. (1983) Microeconomic theory and applications, Little, Brown and Company, Boston

Call, S.T. and Holahan, W.L. (1977) Microeconomics, 2nd edn, Wadsworth, Belmont, California

Cheung, S.N.S., (1980) 'Rush or delay: the effects of rent control on urban renewal in Hong Kong' in R.P. Albon (ed.) Rent control: costs and consequences, op. cit., ch.2, 1980

Clyne, P. (1970) Practical guide to tenancy law, Rydge Publications, Sydney

119

Bibliography

Commission of Inquiry into Poverty (R.F. Henderson, Chairman) (1975) First main report, vols 1 and 2, Commonwealth of Australia, Canberra

Cooper, M.H. and Stafford, D.C. (1975) 'A note on the economic implications of fair rents', Social and Economic Administration, 9, 1, Spring, 26-29

Cooper, M.H. and Stafford, D.C. (1979) 'The economic implications of fair rents' in R.A.P. Leaper (ed.), Health, wealth and happiness, Blackwells, Oxford

Cooper, M.H. and Stafford, D.C. (1980) 'Rent control: the United Kingdom experience' in R.P. Albon (ed.) op. cit., ch. 4, 1980

De Jouvenel, B. (1948) 'No vacancies' reprinted in Verdict on rent control, Institute of Economic Affairs, Readings no. 7, London, 1972

Department of the Environment (1977) The Review of the rent acts - a consultations paper

Frankena, M.W. (1975) 'Alternative models of rent control', Urban Studies, 12, 3, October, 303-308

Fraser Institute (1975) Rent control: a popular paradox, Fraser Institute, Canada

Friedman, M. (1962) Capitalism and freedom, The University of Chicago Press, Chicago

Friedman, M. and Stigler, G. (1946) Roofs or ceilings? Foundation for Economic Education, Inc., Irvington-on-Hudson, New York. Reprinted in Institute of Economic Affairs, Verdict on rent control, Readings No. 7, London, 1972. Reprinted in R.P. Albon (ed.) op. cit., ch. 1, 1980

Greve, J. (1965) Private landlords in England, Occasional

120

Bibliography

Paper on Social Administration, No. 16, Bell

Harrod, R. (1947) Are these hardships necessary?, Rupert Hart-Davis, London

Hayek, F.A. (1930) 'The repercussions of rent restrictions' reprinted in Verdict on rent control, Institute of Economic Affairs, Readings No. 7, London, 1972

Henney, A. (1975) 'The implications of the rent act, 1974' Housing Review, March - April

Hirshleifer, J. (1984) Price theory and applications, 3rd edn. Prentice Hall, Englewood Cliffs, New Jersey

Institute of Public Affairs (1954) 'Rent control', The IPA Review, 8, 3, 73-79. Reprinted in R.P. Albon (ed.), op. cit., Ch. 7 (i), 1980

Lindbeck, A. (1967) 'Rent control as an instrument of housing policy' in A.A. Nevitt (ed.), The economic problems of housing, Macmillan

Lindbeck, A. (1971) The political economy of the new left: an outsider's view, Harper and Row, New York

McCloskey, D. (1985) The applied theory of price, 2nd edn, Macmillan Publishing Co., New York

Maclennan, D. (1978) 'The 1974 rent act - some short run supply effects', The Economic Journal, vol. 88

Maclennan, D. (1980) Housing Economics, Longman

McKenzie, R.B. and Tullock, G. (1978) Modern political economy, McGraw-Hill, New York

Minford, P. Ashton, P. and Peel, M. (1986) The effects of housing distortions on unemployment, Mimeo, Department of Economic and Business Studies,

Bibliography

University of Liverpool

Minford, P. Peel, M and Ashton, P. (1987) The housing morass, Institute of Economic Affairs, Hobart Paperback, no.25, London

Murie, A., (1976) The sale of council houses: a study in social policy, Occ. Paper No. 35, Centre for Urban and Regional Studies, University of Birmingham

Needleman, L. (1965) The economics of housing, Staples, London

Olsen, E.O. (1969a) 'A competitive theory of the housing market', American Economic Review, 59, September, 612-621

Olsen, E.O. (1969b) 'The effects of a simple rent control scheme in a competitive housing market', RAND Corporation, P-4257

Olsen, E.O. (1972) 'An econometric analysis of rent control', Journal of Political Economy, 80, 6, November/December, 1081-1100

Paish, F.W. (1952) 'The economics of rent restriction', Lloyds Bank Review, April. Reprinted in Verdict on rent control, Institute of Economic Affairs, Readings no.7, London, 1972

Paley, B. (1978) Attitudes to letting in 1976 Office of Population Censuses and Surveys, Social Survey Division, JS1091, HMSO

Parish, R.M. (1980), 'Economic effects of Victoria's residential tenancies bill' in R.P. Albon (ed.), op. cit., ch. 12, 1980

Parliament of New South Wales (1961), Report of the Royal Commission of Inquiry on the Landlord and

Bibliography

Tenant (Amendment) Act, 1948, as amended, New South Wales Government Printer, Sydney

Real Estate and Stock Institute of Australia (1975) Rent controls: study of the effects of rent controls in Canberra, Canberra

Ricketts, M. (1986) Lets into leases, Centre for Policy Studies, London

Rydenfelt, S. (1980) 'The rise, fall and revival of Swedish rent control' in R.P. Albon (ed.) op. cit., Ch. 3, 1980

Samuelson, P.A. (1980) Economics, 11th edn, McGraw-Hill Kogakusha, Tokyo

Shreiber, C. and Tabriztchi, S. (1976) 'Rent control in New York City: a proposal to improve resource allocation' Urban Affairs Quarterly, 1, 4, June, 511-522

Stafford, D.C. (1976) 'The final economic demise of the private landlord', Social and Economic Administration, vol. 10, no. 1, Spring

Stafford, D.C. (1978) The economics of housing policy, Croom Helm, London

Todd, J.E. (1986) Recent private lettings 1982-84, HMSO, London

Webster, R.H. (1980) 'Wheeling and dealing under rent control' in R.P. Albon (ed.) Rent control: costs and consequences, op cit. ch. 10, 1980

Wicks, M. (1973) Rented housing and social ownership, Fabian Tract, No. 421, Fabian Society

INDEX

Albon, R.P. 23
Ashton, P. 64, 95
Assured Tenancy Scheme ii

Bank of New South Wales
    59
Begg, D. xnl
board and lodgings 6-7, 11
black market
    empirical evidence 52-3
    theoretical analysis
    18, 50-1, 98
Browning, E.K. xnl
Browning, J.M. xnl
bureaucratic rationing 29,
    49

Call, S.T. xnl
Canberra 50
capital gains taxation 86,
    102
'carrot and stick' 40-1
'chance and favouritism'
    rationing 29, 33, 47, 49
Cheung, S.N.S. vii-viii, 15,
    52-3, 54-5
Clyne, P. 53
collectivism vii, 64-5
Commission of Inquiry into

Poverty (Australia)
    113-14
Committee on Housing in
    Greater London (Milner
    Holland) 74-5
Committee on the Rent
    Acts (Francis) 76-7
Conservative Party i-ii,
    ix-x, xin2, 68, 69, 76-7,
    81, 83-93
Cooper, M.H. 71-3, 98
council housing see local
    authority housing
cross party support 92-3

deadweight losses 18, 19,
    25
decontrol vi, ix-x, 9-12,
    68-9, 92, 98-100,
    105-13, 117
demand and supply analysis
    16-24, 50-1, 70-3,
    115-16
Department of the
    Environment
De Jouvenel, B. 42-3, 45
discrimination v, ix, 18,
    47-53, 77, 98-9
distribution of house space

Index

Landlord and Tenant Act
91, 97
Landlord and Tenant Act
(New South Wales) 53
legal profession vii, 53
Lindbeck, A. 17, 39, 41
local authority housing ii,
vi, x, 18, 63, 75, 84-5,
110-12
London viii, 70, 74-5, 78,
91

McCloskey, D. xn1
McKenzie, R.B. xin1
Maclennan, D. 35-7, 101-3
maintenance and controls
empirical analysis 41-5,
96
theoretical analysis
19-23, 40-1
Malmo 34
Melbourne viii, 44-5
Minford, P. 64, 95, 112
mortgage interest
deductibility vi, 64, 75,
85-6, 110-11, 113
municipalisation x, 95-8
Murie, A. 96-7
Myrdal, G. 1

Needleman, L. 23
neoclassical analysis see
demand and supply
analysis
New York viii

Olsen, E.O. 20

Paish, F.W. 23, 43-4, 62-3,
108

Paley, B. 88
Paris viii, 42-3, 45
Parish, R.M. 115
Parliament of New South
Wales 55n1
Peel, M. 64, 95
political economics of
intervention 3, 8-13,
106-7, 113
property rights vi-vii, 65

quality and controls see
maintenance and
controls

rate of return 3, 32, 75, 89,
95, 102, 117n1
Real Estate and Stock
Institute of Australia
50
Rent Acts i, 35-7, 67-70,
74-81, 83, 88, 90-2,
101-4
rental market 'regulation'
arguments for viii,
12-13, 113-14
theoretical analysis
115-16
Review of the Rent Acts
1977 79-80, 81, 90
Ricketts, M. 67, 107-8, 110
'Robin Hood' redistribution
vi, 108
Rydenfelt, S. 34-5, 41-2

Samuelson, P.A. xn1
San Francisco viii, 27-34,
37, 49, 52
San Francisco Chronicle
28, 33

Index

Printed in the United States
by Baker & Taylor Publisher Services